D1598843

ENDORSEMENTS

As one of the nearly fifty percent of men in our nation who spent a portion of his childhood with no Dad at home, I joined the scores of others who have pressed into the fatherly heart of Dudley Hall in order to receive that invisible, osmosis-like impartation of masculine spirituality that a broken family denied us.

Now, finally, Dudley has put on paper what he's been imparting for all these years—an invitation to let men be men in Christ. *Men in Their Own Skin* does more than point out the dilemma of an overly feminized church; it welcomes men into an unashamed expression of their masculine souls for the great purposes of God in the earth.

Alan Wright
Pastor, author, and host of the daily radio broadcast *Sharing the Light with Alan Wright*

Men in Their Own Skin struck a chord with me. Dudley has given men a roadmap to living a life of significance and purpose. He has challenged me to shed misconceptions that men have in regard to relationships, performance, faith, and most importantly ministry. You will thoroughly enjoy this book.

Chad Hennings
Former Dallas Cowboy, 3-time Super Bowl Champion, former Air Force fighter pilot, and the founder of Wingmen Ministries

I am delighted that Dudley has finally put his counsel to men in book form. He is a man who understands men. When he speaks to men, they know he cares. He has been a vital part of the New Canaan Society team for years. We are pleased to be partners with Dudley and highly recommend this book, *Men in Their Own Skin*.

Jim Lane
Founder of New Canaan Society and former partner with Goldman Sachs

For every grandfather, father, and son who has ever asked the questions, "Why am I here? Where do I fit? How can I meaningfully fulfill my God-given role in this life?"—*Men in Their Own Skin* is a must-read. Being a godly, fulfilled, contented man is a product of being influenced, mentored, and encouraged by godly, fulfilled, contented grandfathers, fathers, and sons. Pass it on through *Men in Their Own Skin*.

Rob Farrell
Farrell Properties

In *Men in Their Own Skin*, Dudley Hall quickly captures the reader's attention and delivers a message that is both insightful and inspiring. Dudley's skills as a Bible teacher and his no-nonsense ability to communicate give men the knowledge and the courage to be leaders for Christ in their homes, in their churches, and in their communities.

Men in Their Own Skin is a powerful, practical book that should be required reading for men who desire to make a difference.

Marc Myers
Myers & Crow Company, Ltd.

Dudley Hall has been a mentor and the spiritual mainstay in my life since 1978. God has given him a ministry that teaches men to be men and to see the kingdom of God at work in their lives and in their sphere of influence. He is a man's man with a kingdom message to men in the marketplace.

Richard Culpepper
Culpepper Development, Inc.

In an era where confusion and compromise shape the contours of a man's values and beliefs, Dudley Hall beckons us back home with the precision that only the infallible Word of God can offer. In his uniquely immutable style, Dudley reminds men that it's not only liberating to live in our own skin, it's a mandate from the Master.

In fact, chapter three alone—"A Man Who Could Marry My Daughter"— is worth the price of the entire book . . . and I don't even have daughters! But I do have four sons who must know who they are in Christ if they're going to be spiritually fit enough to be authentic husbands, fathers, and men of God.

If no improvement is needed in your life, do not read this book. However, if you are like most of us who find ourselves frustrated by a world of mediated messages and insidious information seeking to re-define men as bombastic buffoons not fit for leadership, this book will empower you to be the man God created you to be!

Rick Rigsby, Ph. D.
President, Rick Rigsby Communications and author of
Lessons From a Third Grade Dropout
Chaplain of the Texas A&M Football Team
Former Professor of Communication at Texas A&M University

DUDLEY HALL

MEN
IN THEIR OWN
SKIN

Answering the Call to Confident Manhood

FOREWORD

Men in Their Own Skin is exactly what every man needs to read.
It is written by a man, for men, and it's written in a manly way.

There's no fluff—only stuff. *Real* stuff, the kind of things men truly
need and want to know about as they seek to be the man they always
dreamed of becoming. *Good* stuff, the kind that is helpful and sensible
and will make a difference in how a man lives in today's world. *True*
stuff, the kind that brings freedom and understanding. *Funny* stuff, the
kind that eases the way for us as men to walk out of our blunders with
our self-worth still intact. *Godly* stuff, the kind that connects us to our
Father and helps us learn how much He loves us as men. *Worthwhile*
stuff, the kind that means something when you read it and even more
when you put it into practice. And there's just enough of all this stuff
to not bog you down with endless lists of things to do. In fact, this
book is not about *doing* at all; it's about *being*—being a man in your
own skin, a godly man in today's world.

You will find this book to be personal, practical, and profitable. *Personal*,
for it is polished with stories of real men, just like you, who have grappled
with the same sort of challenges you face as a guy and found answers.
Practical, for it is written in simple, straightforward language, rather
than the typical pontifications usually penned by preachers and pundits
regarded as experts on the subject. Each brief chapter concludes with key
questions and suggestions to help you reach a little deeper in the well, and
find that water of life which refreshes not only you, but others also, who
will want a drink of what you're having. And *profitable*, because you will
be enriched by reading it and applying it to your life. While it is a quick
read, the work it does to reorder your world will last a lifetime.

If men in their own skin will follow the proven tips in this simple,
singular manual, then in a very real and manly way, the Word will once
again become flesh and walk among us. And that will be a beautiful
thing to behold.

James Ryle

TABLE OF CONTENTS

Foreword

CHAPTER
WHY MEN STRUGGLE WITH CHURCH
ONE

I can vividly remember the Sunday the nominating committee announced that every job in the church was filled except the Baptist equivalent of a scout leader. I thought, maybe, just maybe this would be my chance to be taught by a man what it meant to serve God.

You see, when I think back to my earliest memories, I can remember going to church. And whenever I went to church, I was surrounded, instructed, and mentored by women.

When I was in preschool, I went to "Story Hour." It was taught by a 73-year-old widow who baked delicious tea-cakes and quietly read us Bible stories.

When I learned to read, I moved on to "Beginners" class, taught by another lady in the church.

Next came "Primary" class which, interestingly enough, was taught by another woman.

When I graduated to "Intermediates," surprise, surprise . . . it was taught by another woman.

Youth group? Led by a woman.

But there was one glimmer of hope.

A godly man was going to take us camping and fishing, teach us how to tie knots, and maybe even how to carve with a knife. We'd learn Scripture and progress through the ranks of spiritual knighthood.

This was the moment I had waited for. But when the committee asked for a volunteer, all the men in my church looked at the floor. No one stood up for us. No one showed up for us. No one spoke up.

Except the sweet old widow from Story Hour.

But since she couldn't drive, I knew we weren't going to learn spiritual knighthood like a real man while we "played camp" in her living room. I realized if I was going to learn *from a man* what the Bible had to say to men, it wasn't going to happen in my church.

When I left for college, I had never been taught in church by a man except from the pulpit. But even then, I didn't feel like the pastor talked to me like a "man." I knew there were things he wasn't telling me — wild, daring, passionate, powerful, important things that were at the heart of who God made me.

I greatly appreciate that sweet widow who loved God and served us, through teaching us God's Word during Story Hour. I'm grateful for all the women who took the time to point me and other young men toward a Christ-centered life. But I have wondered for a long time why the men didn't feel like they were suited for those roles.

During more than forty years of ministry, I've encountered dozens of men who share this experience. They wanted to be challenged, to experience "the band of brothers," to be formed and strengthened by the camaraderie of the men in their community. They looked for that experience in their church . . . but they couldn't find it.

These were good men who loved God. They needed instruction. They needed someone to show them what it looks like when a warrior prays or when a hero worships.

One of these men told me this story:

> In the town I came from, I worked cattle with a big group of men. It was hard work, but the camaraderie alone was worth it. The only rank out there that was recognized was earned by practiced skill and lots of sweat. Guys were playing pranks on each other, and the jokes and stories were more entertaining than anything you'd see at the movies. Lots of grunting and laughing were mixed with a carefully plotted strategy to get the job done. These were men at work.
>
> Everything changed on Sunday. I hardly recognized the men from work. They were all washed up and looking good in their "Sunday Best." I appreciated that change, but the one I wasn't ready for was in their demeanor. They looked intimidated. Those same men who would face down a 2,000 lb. bull with nothing but a rope looked scared and confused. What was going on?
>
> What happens to men when they go to church? Does someone demand that men leave their masculinity at the door? To be honest, the few men who did participate in the church service looked pretty domesticated. They weren't like the guys working the cattle. I know — not every man has to work outside, spit on the ground, and become

sun-tanned and wrinkled. But you know what I mean . . . they didn't look like they were enjoying what they were doing. They looked somehow out of place. I'm sure they loved God and were sincere, but they didn't look like they had laughed much. I doubt they could tell a good story, or if they even had one to tell. I wondered if they could make a tough decision if a fellow was in trouble and something risky had to be done quickly.

I knew that some of the men had not been in church much, and I wondered if they even knew what was going on. They didn't speak *Christianese*, so they didn't understand some of what was being said. These would not be the words these guys were accustomed to using during the week. We all probably need to learn a few more words, and surely we need to know the meaning of the important ones that define our faith, but it almost felt like being a visitor in a club where only old members were welcome. It was evident that the men I knew felt out of place and probably would not be there if it weren't for the prompting of their women. Speaking of whom, the ladies looked right at home . . . heads up, talking, teaching, praying, and singing. It looked sorta like a women's club with some uncomfortable men attending.

Not all church services alienate men, but too many do. What makes a man feel intimidated in a worship service? I think three things contribute to intimidating men in church:

they are *paralyzed spiritually, feminized socially, and demoralized religiously.*

First, many men are *paralyzed spiritually.* What do I mean here? Erroneously, men have believed that they will never measure up to what is expected of them as men and as Christians. All they know is what they're "not allowed" to do. Fear of failure locks them up. They could never be as spiritual as their women or the minister at church. They don't know the Scriptures, the songs, or what they're supposed to say or do. They can have all the confidence in the world being a man at their job, working on a car, or playing sports, but they have no idea what it looks like to be a real man in church.

They are condemned by their moral failures because they've never given and received true forgiveness. So they have concluded that no matter how sorry they are, they are disqualified for full fellowship and useful service. After failing so many times to live the expected holy life, they have decided that they need not try again. They are resigned to be the unspiritual but practical parts of the church. They find some amount of significance in doing the traditional things that men do, like ushering, counting money, and serving on boards that make decisions about fiscal matters.

Am I overstating this? Is every man paralyzed spiritually in their church? No, but I've heard way too many stories to ignore. There are a lot who are. It doesn't have to be this way.

When a man feels disqualified from leading in the church because of his guilt from the past, it only gets worse if he's a bottom-line kind of guy. Men tend to break things down into categories. Black or white. In or out. Sacred or secular.

You know the drill. Spiritual work is what is done relating to ecclesial issues like worship, missions, evangelism, Bible study, prayer, charitable work, etc. Secular work is what is done by the "uncalled" laymen. It relates to marketplace stuff: making profits, building cities, military, government, science, education, etc.

The inevitable conclusion is that the ordinary men are to make the money to fund the ecclesial work. Those blessed enough to be in ecclesial ministry get to do the spiritual work and enjoy a special position with God. This creates problems as it creates a gap between the pastors and ministers and the rest of the men in the church. Both sides act like they can't relate to each other, and when they do, the laymen feel especially uneasy and uncertain. And when you're uncertain, you're not going to be honest and work with your pastor on the "big stuff" in life.

This separation comes from the misguided idea that you have to be called to be in ecclesial work, but the other work needs no call or assignment from God. It's just stuff that has to be done; it's not sacred or holy. In extreme cases, it can even be viewed as part of the sinful world system that cannot be sanctified. It exists only to support the church's programs and mission. But as we'll see, all work is sacred. The word for work comes from the same Hebrew word as "worship." God created all of us to worship Him through our work, no matter what our job is.

When you don't understand this, your work feels insignificant, which often leads to a poor work ethic. If you're just going through the motions and getting a paycheck, why does it matter? But if you know that your work honors God when it's done from a heart that wants to please Him, you'll be more productive, your work ethic will improve, and you'll end up doing better in your workplace.

When work is seen as an act of worship to God, meaning comes to EVERY marketplace.

Now let's deal with the *feminized socially* issue.
In America over the past forty years, there has been a concerted effort to give women any role they want. The thinking behind this is that while men have been dominant and domineering, women have just as much to offer as men. In this view, women can be Navy SEALs, NFL quarterbacks, and even fathers, just as well or better than a man.

This process has left many men uncertain about whether it's okay to be a strong man. A new picture of masculinity as "sensitive, caring, and passive," has been promoted as an ideal. This man is more poet than warrior, more dancer than athlete, more follower than leader.

It doesn't have to be either or. It's critical that we understand the issue and don't overreact. God has created the masculine and feminine to compliment and complete His image in mankind. The masculine and feminine traits of mankind all come from the same God who created all men and women in His image. The separation was to be a blessing to mankind. Men and women will always benefit when both are contributing to a family, a community, and a church.

The war was between the serpent and the seed of woman. It was not supposed to be between the man and woman. We will never win if we continue to perceive the battle as between masculine and feminine. It is the perversion of both that we want to address.

It is God's desire for us to recover the true intent of both so that we can enjoy His creation to the fullest. Maybe these passages from Paul's letter to Thessalonica will illustrate the differences in masculine and feminine purposes.

> But we were gentle among you, like a nursing mother taking care of her own children. So, being affectionately desirous of you, we were ready to share with you not only the gospel of God but also our own selves, because you had become very dear to us (1 Thessalonians 2:7-8).

> For you know how, like a father with his children, we exhorted each one of you and encouraged you and charged you to walk in a manner worthy of God, who calls you into his own kingdom and glory (1 Thessalonians 2:11-12).

Notice that both of these are genuine emphases in the ministry of the Spirit of God. The mother-like nurture of God is shown through self-sacrifice and efforts to make the atmosphere suitable for growth and health. Nurture is fundamental to our survival and growth. But there is also the father-like destiny that is needed if we are to become what God designed.

Both of these roles should be strong in every church and in every home.

Every man needs to be called into manhood and destiny by another man. These moments define and shape us.

I can still recall one of these defining moments in my own life. It was a Saturday morning, and I was sleeping in late. I heard the screen door open, and before I even heard his voice, I knew who it was and I knew what he wanted.

He didn't yell, but I could hear his strong voice through the floor. "Where's the boy?" my father asked.

I couldn't make out my mother's response, but I had been out late with my friends the night before. The fact that I was still in bed told me that she had been compassionately pleading my case. My Dad wasn't convinced.

"Sleep late hell," he replied to her attempt to persuade him. His voice was growing in intensity, but more importantly, I could hear his heavy footsteps coming closer. In moments my door opened, and my time to rest was officially over.

"Let's go. We're burning daylight. You know this is our day to work together!"

As I got dressed and made my way outside for a long day of hard work, I wondered what it would be like to live in a home like some of my friends. Dreams of sleeping until noon, doing whatever I wanted, and avoiding discipline seemed so appealing back then. But now, looking back I am so grateful that my Dad loved me enough to be strong, to challenge me to be great, and to instill values of hard work and discipline in me.

It made a man out of me.

We've been conditioned to side with Mom at the expense of Dad. But both my Mom and Dad were expressing their God-given roles. The true feminine-mother spirit is focused on nurture while caring about destiny. The true masculine-father spirit is focused on destiny while caring about nurture. There is a lot of emphasis on the need for nurturing children, but there's not enough focus on calling them in their destiny. Both girls and boys are starving for a sense of destiny. Many of them have been nurtured to the point of being pampered. Everything has been done for them by people who wanted their best, but were in fact crippling them. God didn't just make us for "play dates." He created us to handle responsibility, to overcome adversity, to face great challenges, and to succeed.

My son and I lead a summer program called LEADERSHIP EXPEDITION for young men 16-25 years of age. It is designed to call leadership out of young men. It is not a typical church camp. It is tough. Every moment of the day is designed to call them up to their destiny. They learn the value of decision making. Choices have consequences, and they are real. They learn to make choices that affect others, as they work in teams to accomplish goals.

They work, sweat, struggle, and some even vomit, as they push themselves to discover what is really inside. At the conclusion we ask for an evaluation, and invariably they suggest we make it tougher. They like being called up!

This kind of challenge, mentoring, and formation will change your life. Some of these men are now leading agents of change in this culture. They are men comfortable in their skin.

Generally, the church has focused on the nurture side of ministry that promotes mercy and kindness. All of us need the mercy of God first shown like a mother's willingness to reach out and care for her child. But babies grow up.

There comes a time when we need the exhortation of the father's insistence to become more than we are. We need the father to challenge us, to push us, to refuse to allow us to drift or become stagnant. That is mercy too.

Like spoiled children, too many church members demand that their "felt needs" are met. Sermons are critiqued like a performance. Choosing a church becomes like choosing your favorite place to shop, and we all know that the customer is *always* right. The overfed and destiny-starved congregation can never get satisfied. They demand more excitement and comfort, while the church leaders compete with the other churches for attendees.

In this environment, many men feel out of place. They wonder why it takes half the year to plan a church "drama" or why so much of the budget is spent on décor. They even feel guilty that they don't see such things as important.

With so many big problems in the world and major challenges in their own community, they wonder if their church is actually making a difference. They want to know that it matters. They want to know that the effort, the money, and the time they gave made a difference.

They try to change so that they can enjoy the corporate worship times like their wives. But honestly some of it reinforces their feelings of inferior spirituality. They wonder; "Why can't I get into it like my wife?"

Recently, I was in a conference setting with a strong sense of genuine worship. The singing was lively. People were moving to the rhythm of the music, and hands were raised all over the room as people worshipped the Lord. I looked over the congregation; it seemed that everyone there was focused and singing from their hearts. I thought it was unusually wonderful.

I was not ready for what happened next. The leader asked us all to turn to the person next to us, hold their hand, look them in the eye, and sing the chorus to them.

You want me to do what?

Now, I've been in ecclesial ministry for forty-plus years, and I've had many opportunities to worship in all kinds of different ways, but even I felt really uncomfortable. I could genuinely say, "I love you with the love of the Lord" as the song suggested, but looking into the eyes of a stranger while holding hands was not something I could do without much distraction.

The point is, I don't think I'll ever get to the place where that is a comfortable act of worship. I don't even want to get to that place. Does that mean I'm an insensitive worshipper? I don't think so.

Maybe some women could do that easily, but not many men. I happened to look around during the chorus, and judging by the panicked and awkward looks on their faces, most of the men felt like me. They wanted to run away. Most did after the service ended. I wonder if they ever went back.

Situations like this create lasting memories in men. They'll do whatever they have to not to go through it again. But worse, it leads men to take a passive role in church leadership. If that's what it does to you, they don't want any part of it. And why would they?

Finally, men are *demoralized religiously*. It looks hopeless to so many men. They have given up on the church as a vehicle for life-giving relationships with God and others. They respect it too much to condemn it, but have chosen to find their spirituality elsewhere.

They can never measure up to the models of nurture that define the work of the church. Mother Teresa and Francis of Assisi are beyond their realistic dreams. They need a more realistic model of what a man of God looks like. They want someone they can relate to, someone they understand, and someone who faces and overcomes the same challenges they face.

They want examples of real men who serve God.

They also feel somewhat used. Courted by church leaders who need the finances to fund the programs, they feel jilted when it comes to any sense of ownership of vision.

Jeff came by my office a few weeks ago. He looked like something was really bothering him.

"I need to talk, but I don't know where to start, and I feel shame in just bringing up the subject."

"OK, you didn't take off work to come here and look pitiful," I said. "What's up?"

"Well, I may just be greedy, but I'm bothered by what I feel about my giving to the church. I don't want to be on staff . . . and I appreciate everything our church does for the members and the community. I don't have to know everything that goes on in the decision making . . . but I feel like a cash cow.

"I feel like the only value I have to the church is the money I make and send. I'm sorry. I need help. I should give happily and never look back, I guess . . ."

This was no sudden outburst. I could tell Jeff had been praying and wrestling through this for quite some time.

"Then I get requests for support from many other ministries," he continued. "They seem legitimate, and honestly, they seem to get more bang for the buck. I mean, some of them are making a dramatic difference in places where our church does not go. I know I'm as spoiled as anyone, but it just seems that we spend a lot of money on ourselves for our own comfort."

He was on a roll, and he showed no signs of slowing down.

"I was taught that I should tithe to my local church and never question what's done with it. It seems sacrilegious to even suggest something different, but I wonder. Is sending money the only way I can serve God? Shouldn't I be concerned with quality and efficiency in the church's ministry? Shouldn't I expect the church to equip me to spread the kingdom on earth?"

Like a lot of men, Jeff is what I call "demoralized religiously." Despite his best efforts, he's struggling to trust his church. He's not sure if they represent his heart and his passion or if they're simply filling a role.

They haven't given up on the idea of church, but they are struggling with *their* church.

In the following pages we will address some of Jeff's questions and find solutions that will train and empower men to be who God made them.

FOR FURTHER STUDY

1. Do you believe that women are more interested in church than men? If so, why?

2. Have you experienced both the "mother" and "father" ministry described in 1 Thessalonians 2:7-12? What programs in churches have you seen that specifically meet these needs?

3. What men in the Bible do you admire the most? What men in history do you admire? Why?

4. What would you say is your biggest obstacle in being a fully spiritual man?

CHAPTER
WHAT EVERY MAN WANTS
TWO

A friend handed me a book about the life of "Mister Rogers" and said it would help me get in touch with my feminine side. I thanked him for the book but said, "When I want to get in touch with my feminine side, I roll over. I married her."

I later heard a popular comedian use the same line. Honestly, I didn't copy him. But obviously we both came to the same conclusion. Men don't want to know how to be more like women. What they really want is to know how to be men.

A real man knows who he is. His identity comes from God, and he passionately pursues God's plan for his life.

I actually did enjoy the book because in so many ways, Fred Rogers was a real man. Most people don't realize that he was an ordained Presbyterian minister who loved God. He was committed to the vision God gave him to encourage and teach children. He gave his life to the cause and in the process, inspired millions. He knew who he was.

Unfortunately, this is becoming increasingly rare. Men of all ages, from different backgrounds, all across the country are confused. They don't know who they really are. They're not sure who they're supposed to be. And when a man doesn't know who he is, he listens to all the wrong voices concerning his identity.

We've been told all men are animals obsessed with sex and violence. We've been told that a man's worth is determined by who he sleeps with, what kind of car he drives, and how much money he has. Fulfillment lies in the next conquest.

We're actually being sold conflicting views of manhood at the same time. On one hand, we've been told that real men are emotionless loners who are too strong to let anyone in. On the other hand, we've been told that a real man follows his feelings wherever they lead him regardless of the consequences.

When men are defined by popular culture, ad campaigns, locker rooms, and the local bar, the results are disastrous. They're left confused, frustrated, depressed, and angry, hurting themselves and those around them in the process.

TV programs continue to generally portray men at their worst. From Archie Bunker to Homer Simpson, times have changed, but Dad is still an idiot. Helpless without Mom, he's more pitiful than ever.

Reality television has given us no shortage of immature, deceitful men who care only about themselves and will abuse anyone in their way to get what they want.

The stylish, intelligent men are often portrayed pursuing "alternative lifestyles." Men are bombarded with images of failure and suggestions toward being more like their feminine counterparts.

But what is masculinity anyway? Did God make a mistake in making men and women different? Is the egalitarian spirit of our age going to succeed in erasing the lines of distinction between men and women?

No matter what the court of public opinion decides, every man is created with God-given desires that define who He is. They may be hidden, but deep down, they're there. They were put there by God. They may have been obscured by lies and the latest trends, but they are there waiting to be uncovered and released.

Proverbs 20:5 says, *"The purpose in a man's heart is like deep water, but a man of understanding will draw it out."*

In the deep waters of every man's heart, he wants to **show up.** He doesn't want to miss his moment in history. He desperately wants to be a part of something significant, something greater than himself. This desire causes men to join teams, the military, a great company, or even a gang.

If he can't find something really significant, he will make something significant out of the ridiculous. I noticed recently on a sport's channel, a wood sander's competition. Yes, they were racing the sanders that carpenters use to finish wood. I can just see it now: Ole Jed with his trophy sitting on his TV while he and his grandsons watch reruns of *Gunsmoke*.

"What's that grandpa?"

"Oh, that's what I'm famous for, boys. I had the fastest sander in the world."

It makes you laugh, but it gives him pride. It validates him. It marks a significant moment in his life. Others might think it strange, but something deep inside feels better because on one Saturday afternoon in June, he won the sander race. The boys look at each other with awe. "Grandpa is a winner."

This longing of the heart to be significant, was put there by God. In fact, it reflects God's original design for men. God created men to lead in their families and in their communities. He created men to discover and communicate His truth for their wives, their families, and their workplace. He created men to defend those truths against the schemes of hell filled with every imaginable lie that deceives and destroys people.

Men were created to declare and defend the truth. And when they don't they struggle with insignificance.

Once they've been redeemed by God, they want to do it. It is at the core of who they are. It shouldn't surprise us to realize the strategy of hell is to do whatever it takes to deter men from this calling. When men fail to walk with God, to declare His truth, and to advance His kingdom, they give themselves up to lifeless pursuits that fail to live up to their high calling.

No matter what it may look like on the outside, deep down they know they're not real men. They're not all that they were created to be.

They've failed, and they know it.

The good news is, success is possible. Men can live this way.

The godly man who is present and engaged in all of his God-given responsibilities radically transforms every environment he enters.

When this kind of man shows up, he wins. Not every battle, but in the end he wins the war.

When we refuse to be defeated by accusations, fraudulent models of manhood, and the empty pursuits of the world, we march forward into victory. God has given us the victory through Jesus. When we follow our great leader, there's no enemy, no ambush, no attack that we cannot overcome. When every shot from hell has been fired and the smoke clears, we will be standing.

Maybe we didn't know why we showed up or what to do when we did show up, but we showed up. God's not asking us to have all the answers or to understand exactly why things happened the way they did. He's asking us to obey, to persevere, and no matter what happens, to keep showing up.

God's plans NEVER fail. He stands sovereign over time, orchestrating history to ensure that His purpose will be achieved, regardless of the choices of mankind. Remember that even Israel's rejection of the Messiah did not stop redemption from being implemented right on time.

Next, deep in the heart of every man is the longing to **stand up**. He wants to be counted as being *for* something. He wants a heroic cause worth laying down his life. Being a follower of Christ has never been about what a man is against but what a man is for.

Man is a warrior and a defender by nature. When a man comes to faith in Jesus Christ he finally understands this nature that has been redeemed. He no longer has to look for battles to fight. He is aware that he has been privileged to participate in the battle of the ages . . . and the victory has already been decided.

> Finally, be strong in the Lord and in the strength of his might. Put on the whole armor of God, that you may be able to stand against the schemes of the devil. For we do not wrestle against flesh and blood, but against the rulers, against the authorities, against the cosmic powers over this present darkness, against the spiritual forces of evil in the heavenly places (Ephesians 6:10-12).

Notice that our greatest act of courage is simply "to stand." Bowing or kneeling always represents submission. But standing in the face of the enemy is a defiant declaration that your allegiance lies elsewhere.

It's the four young Hebrew men refusing to bow to King Nebuchadnezzar.

It's Peter and John standing trial when they were arrested for preaching the Gospel, boldly declaring that they cannot stop speaking about what they'd seen.

It's Martin Luther refusing to back down, defiantly proclaiming, "Here I stand; I can do no other." God has placed us in an enviable position, and the forces of darkness try to get us to abandon it. The enemy wants us to sit down, to stay silent and to do nothing as he ravages our homes, our communities, and our nations. But we are in Christ, a very good place to stand. We are ambassadors of heaven, another good position. We are sons of God. Now that is really something.

Because of who we are in Christ and the position God has given us, we act out of our being and behave out of our belief. In other words, we are free only when we are doing what is consistent with our identity. If you are a dog, barking is the expected expression of your nature. If you are a servant, you express this identity through your service. If you are a minister (as all believers are), you find ministry comes out of you without even trying. If you are a giver (all sons of God have His giving nature), you will be frustrated if you aren't giving. You've gotten the point.

Recently, I was talking about this with a friend who was frustrated because he couldn't find his place in ministry. He had tried working on staff at a church, and that didn't work. He had been on mission trips, hoping God would call him to a specific country and mission, but he never heard anything.

Now he was concluding that he should just slink back into insignificance, sit on the bench and watch the significant players play the game. His view of "ministry" was too small.

"Are you a believer in Jesus Christ?" I asked.

"Of course I am," he responded.

"Then you are a minister no matter where you are," I continued. "Tell me what you did yesterday."

He wasn't convinced. "I worked all day," he insisted. "I know you'll say that's ministry, but it's indirect ministry. I want to do more direct ministry."

I could tell that his perspective only allowed him to see ministry as something owned by pastors or missionaries. I wasn't giving up. "What time did you go to work?" I inquired.

"Well, I was a little late because my neighbor has been sick, and I mowed his lawn," he responded. He completely missed the significance of what he had just said.

He knew better, so I laid it on thick. "Duh!"

His perception of ministry didn't allow him to accept it, and he continued to dismiss what he had done. "Well, that's a good deed I guess, but everybody does that kind of thing. And when he's well, he won't need me to help him again. It's not like you can have a 'lawn mowing ministry.'"

It was so obvious. He was standing and serving in the place God had put him. That's what ministry is all about. I wanted him to appreciate the simple yet significant way that God had used him.

"Don't you see!?" I exclaimed. "It's so natural that you don't even notice that you're serving out of your heart. You didn't get up yesterday thinking about ministry. You just saw a neighbor in need and you met it. What else are you already doing that allows you to give your life away?"

Take note of the positions God has already given us as Christian men and find a way to stand there. Standing will prove to be a source of great fulfillment. After all, we were created to stand fast and defend the place God has given us. The deep yearning of our soul is to stand up.

Finally, deep down every man wants to *speak up.* He wants to be heard about things that matter. When this need is not met properly, a man will either say what he thinks people want to hear or nothing at all.

But you can only hold it in for so long. Have you noticed that old men like to gather around the coffee shop or chess board or the whittler's bench and talk politics, religion, sports, and women? Listen sometime, and you'll hear that each one has his say about something.

Every man wants to add his two cents. He may be quiet for a long time until his subject comes up. But when his passion is brought up, he'll speak his piece. If he's one of the men that stopped speaking, he'll try to make up for lost time by weighing in on the issues he shied away from before.

Again, God created men with this desire. Our mouths and our words were made to honor God. He has made Jesus the theme of history and the subject of every issue that matters. Each man has a perspective of Him based on his own experience, temperament, and training. When he is intimidated into refusing to speak up for Jesus, he feels compromised and again slinks back to the spectator's bench.

But there is good news about speaking up. God will back up His word. Seriously, when we speak according to His Word, the same power that created the universe authenticates it. It was His Word that created the universe, and it was His Word that redeemed it.

We are privileged to use such a supernatural tool. It is not recognized by the deluded masses who mock its simplicity, but there is miraculous power in the words of the man who believes God. Our challenge is to discover His Word in each issue and say it with confident love.

A man speaks with confidence when he knows what he's talking about. In order to speak the truth of God's Word, we've got to spend time studying it. We have to become close to Him to speak with authority *about* Him. When we have a strong relationship with Jesus, we won't be reluctant to speak about it.

Men who know and love football have no trouble talking about football. They'll do it whenever, wherever. Have you ever talked to a passionate hunter? He has more stories and detailed knowledge of the hunt than you could possibly sit and listen to. A great fisherman will fascinate you with an unending stream of stories, featuring every kind of fish in all kinds of conditions.

In the same way, the man who knows and walks with God is always ready to speak of the greatness of his God.

Some men are intimidated and slow to speak because they don't have all the answers. Or they're afraid that they're not eloquent or gifted enough to say the right thing. The excellence of the message should be matched as much as possible with excellent presentation, but God will use our bumbling but sincere efforts as He confounds the wise of the world system.

While I was a college student, I was part of an evangelistic team that taught high school kids how to share their faith. I had always used the "Roman Road" approach to witnessing—a method that takes several verses from the book of Romans to explain the Gospel and invite people to receive salvation.

But someone had just given me a new pamphlet, "The Four Spiritual Laws." (Yeah, I know that was a long time ago.) I thought I would try using that method in my training and took two students along with me as we went house to house.

The first stop was at an older man's home. He invited us in when I told him we were training to share our faith. I jumped right in to the four spiritual laws. I got the first one down: "God loves you and has a wonderful plan for your life." He asked a couple of questions, and I forgot the sequence of the laws. I began to ramble trying to think of what the booklet had said. I got the third law before the second and then bungled the fourth one.

Finally, I looked at the man pathetically and asked, "Would you like to receive Jesus as your Savior and Lord?"

I was sure he was as confused as I was, and I fully expected him to respectfully decline. Instead, he said, "Son this is the first time I have ever understood the gospel. You have made it as plain as day. I do want to pray with you."

That was the last thing I expected him to say. I was sure he had misunderstood, so I spent several minutes going back over the seriousness of becoming a Christian. He assured me he knew what he was doing and intended to trust Jesus alone for the salvation he had always wanted.

I realized right then that it wasn't the quality of the messenger that determined the response. It's God's Spirit that leads men to repentance, not our persuasive words. All the glory belongs to Him. But if I was not willing to show up, stand up, and speak up, I would not have this story to tell.

We live in a culture that discourages speaking up on issues of disagreement. The problem is that people tend to disagree on issues of ultimate importance. Political correctness teaches people to value sensitivity and inoffensive speech more than truth.

People aren't fat anymore; they're "horizontally-gifted."

People aren't lazy either; they're "motivationally-challenged."

People don't sin anymore; they're all "basically good people" who do what seems right to them in the moment.

Somehow all paths lead to the same God, even if some paths allow you to have multiple wives, some charge you tens of thousands of dollars to be enlightened, and others lead you to crash planes into skyscrapers to kill people to honor this same God.

The hypocrisy of featuring a perverted *tolerance* as the ultimate virtue makes real men angry. True tolerance is not the result of everyone agreeing. Tolerance means you respect someone who has a very different perspective. This perverted tolerance forces people to agree and even endorse things they detest to promote a false peace. According to this system, the only acceptable absolute is *there are no absolutes*.

Men secretly admire those who dare to stand and say what is true about God, sin, truth, and war, even when it gets them in trouble with the culture. This doesn't mean that you attack people. You attack the lies. It's not popular, but something deep down in a man wants to draw a line in the sand and refuse to move from it.

This willingness to stand unapologetically and undeterred for something causes men to rally around insignificant things like sports talk radio, stand-up comedians, and over-the-top political pundits.

No man wants to be suppressed by self-appointed language detectives and popular opinion. They feel they are going to burst if they don't speak, and speak they will. Like William Wilberforce in his generation, there are men who will change their culture because they cannot hold it in. They're willing to give their lives to see the cause of Christ advance over the earth, whether or not they see the results in their lifetime. They're not just living for the moment; they're living for history. They are getting ready now for their moment because they know that it's coming.

The words of Todd Beamer echo in the hearts of men in this generation, especially in America. As a passenger on the hijacked flight United #93, he discovered that the terrorists weren't interested in ransom. They were going to use the plane as a weapon to destroy a strategic American target to inspire fear and panic and promote their twisted cause.

Knowing that his actions would cost him his life, *he showed up, stood up, and spoke up.*

We only know two words he spoke in that moment, "Let's roll!" But his actions spoke so much more. They boldly declared truth to the deceived men carrying out their diabolical plan: You can hijack my plane, but you can't hijack my manhood.

Todd's words are now a rallying cry for every man who discovers there is something worse than dying: never actually living.

Don't live a safe, selfish life. Don't be defined by the culture. Don't chase fulfillment in empty pursuits.

Be a man comfortable in your own skin. Be the man that God created you to be. Find your purpose in Him. You can do this.

"Let's roll!"

FOR FURTHER STUDY

1. When was the last time that you *showed up*? What obstacles or challenges keep you from showing up?

2. When was the last time you *stood up*? What prevents you from doing this more?

3. What happened the last time you had the chance to *speak up*? How did that experience affect your willingness to do it again?

4. Do you know who God has called you to be? How are you pursuing God's plan for your life?

CHAPTER

A MAN WHO COULD MARRY MY DAUGHTER

THREE

All it takes is one pink blanket, and something supernatural happens in the heart of a father. There is nothing quite like the special bond that a father shares with his daughter.

You know at first glance that she's a beauty queen. And as you hold her for the first time, the idea of laying down your life for her seems easy and right. Visions of playing dolls and having tea-parties take on more excitement than ball games or fishing trips.

From the moment your eyes meet, she forever wins a special place in your heart.

In the flood of emotions the new father experiences those first few days, sooner or later he thinks about boys.

It usually sounds a little like this: *"Why, I'll cripple any idiotic, hairy legged, half-witted boy who comes snooping around my house. This girl is precious. She's a princess. She is not just any girl to be handled and hounded. She is my daughter. It will take a real man to attract her, and he better have his act together if he expects to get my permission to marry her."*

Yep. I know the feeling. So what kind of man could qualify to marry my daughter?

There are lots of questions to ask a would-be suitor.

You could have a couple of consultants join you. Smith and Wesson. Or perhaps Remington and Glock. You might even consider hooking him up to a polygraph, a lie-detector, when you're interrogating . . . err talking with him.

Once you set the right tone, you could get to the questions.

"What do *character* and *integrity* mean to you? Where does your sense of right and wrong come from?"

"Where did you go to school, and what degree did you earn? How are you going to provide for my daughter? Tell me about your career and your plans for the future."

"What is your family like? What was your environment like growing up? How is your relationship with family now?" (After all when two people marry they are connecting two histories . . . of families, not just individuals.)

Finances, sex, and religion are usually the three big issues in marriage conflict, so you need to talk about these issues early and often.

But before I give my blessing to any potential suitor, there are four things about him that I have to know for certain.

1) SECURE IN HIS IDENTITY

First, he has to know who he is. The identity of a real man is rooted in what God says about Him. God's Word defines him, it frames his understanding of the meaning of life, and it is the single source of his self-worth.

If this man is trying to satisfy the culture's demands in order to validate himself, he'll never be secure. And his insecurity will be disastrous for my daughter. This security comes from a father who trains a son and calls him into manhood. Because this is becoming increasingly rare, this role can be substituted by a community of God-fearing men. It's not the ideal, but it can still be effective.

You can't get it from advertisements. You can't get it watching TV or movies. You can't find it in a locker room, the first time you cuss, take a dip, get drunk, get in a fight, or have sex. It doesn't come from buying your first house or making your first million.

Every man needs another man to show him who he is in Christ. AND before he can marry my daughter, *this man* has to know who he is in Christ.

Our name says so much about us, yet none of us get to choose our name. I certainly would not have chosen "Dudley" if given the chance. At times I felt like "Sue" from Johnny Cash's song about a boy with an unusual name. But unlike Sue, I have come to make peace with Dudley. I have spent a lifetime giving meaning to what it represents.

Someone else names us before we have a chance to give ourselves distinct meaning. That's why it's very important that a boy understands who he is, the significance of his name, and what it means to be a man.

If no one leads him, when he's constantly being reminded that he is a sexual being defined by his exploits, he'll view that as a primary source of his identity. He'll use women and treat them like objects to demonstrate his significance.

If he is applauded for his reckless and rebellious attitude toward life, and excused because he is "just being a boy," then he will continue to defy authority. Our prisons are filled with middle-aged "boys" still trying to get someone to recognize their manhood.

If he is put down because he wasn't "the best" for mom, dad, coach, or girlfriend, he will define himself strictly on the results of his performance. When you have to be the best to be loved, you'll cheat in school, at work, in elections, and anything else you participate in. Stories of corruption topple "heroes" in neighborhoods, communities, and our nation on a daily basis.

If he is affirmed solely on the basis of his athletic ability and excused from other responsibilities because of it, he will just be an athlete—even when he's too old to play. Recreation leagues across America are filled with aging athletes who're clinging to sports because they don't know how to be anything else.

If told that his sensitive nature and passion for the arts are evidence that he was born "different" than other men, he may accept an alternate sexual identity. When a young man feels misunderstood and different, anyone who makes a concerted effort to understand him becomes powerfully persuasive. An alternative lifestyle feels like a small price to pay for a genuine sense of belonging.

Of course, some would disagree and insist that they're "self-made men." They form, shape, and determine their own destiny. They chose their own identity. They don't need anyone else to lead them. But that is actually arrogance that befits a fool. You can't name yourself, and in the end, you can't define yourself either.

We are by creation social beings, and our identity comes through our relationships with others and the world around us. We learn who we are as we fit into our family, our community, and hopefully in the body of Christ.

In my mind, I believe I am the quarterback of the team. That might change when the rest of the team shows up, though.

When does a boy become a man?

Is it when he becomes a certain age? No, we all mature at different rates.

Is it when he can produce offspring? That declares him a male, but not necessarily a man.

Is it when he gets a job and supports himself? Many employers would argue that too many are still boys looking for independence.

Is it when he gets married? I bet a lot of wives would disagree with that!

When does a boy become a man? The answer might surprise you: *It is when a father or group of fathers tells him he is a man.* It can't be conferred upon a boy by another boy or by himself. And as much as she may wish otherwise, it cannot be done by a mother.

This is why I believe it is so important for fathers to have a specific time to call boys into manhood. When fathers fail to call boys into manhood, boys don't become men. The

problem is grown-up boys end up hurting themselves
and those around them, spiritually, emotionally, and
often physically.

Since the mid 1980s I have been hosting an annual father/son
retreat where men are instructed in biblical masculinity and
given an opportunity to go through a ceremony calling the
boys into manhood by the fathers. It continues to be one of
the most powerful events our ministry leads.

No one is left out from experiencing this defining moment.
Those who cannot have their natural fathers present still
have the community of fathers who recognize their identity
and affirm them as men.

Over the years I've received an overwhelming number of
reports of dramatic changes in the lives of these men. Fathers
marvel at the newfound confidence and responsibility in their
sons. This experience is so moving, the older men who are
participating in the community of fathers will often ask, with
tear-filled eyes, if they can go through the ceremony too.

It takes deep conviction to move men to this type of honesty.
Recently one of the men put it this way, "I am 47 years old,
and no one ever told me I was a man. I have tried to be a
good man, but I wish someone had told me earlier what it
meant and recognized me as a man."

So if the male who is seeking my daughter doesn't yet know
he is a man, we'll have to talk more before there can be any
more serious discussion about a wedding. Boys don't make
good husbands.

A man who could marry my daughter or yours needs to be confident in his person. All women deserve a man who at least knows that. If he doesn't know that he is a man and that he is a product of the cross of Jesus Christ, he will have a tough time being the confident leader, generous provider and fearless protector that every wife hopes for in a husband.

2) SOLID IN HIS INTEGRITY

The second requirement is simple. This man must do what he says. In other words, he must be a man of integrity. He can only do that if he has discovered how to live from the inside out. All of us eventually live out of our being. We are not what we do; we *do* what we *are*.

The man who lives a lie, who deceptively "plays a role" different from his true nature, will frustrate himself and offend others. That's where the word *hypocrite* comes from; he's an actor on a stage who wears a mask that hides his true self. And if his act includes his spiritual life, he is a wolf in sheep's clothing.

But if a man's heart is right with God, if his mind is being renewed by the Word, and if he's obeying God and following His plan, he'll bear great fruit in all of his relationships.

All of this starts with believing and obeying. In Matthew 7:17, Jesus says that every "good tree" bears "good fruit." He promised that we could spot the bad tree, the wolf in sheep's clothing, by the fruit in his life.

Bad fruit comes from wrong thoughts, which lead to sinful attitudes and ultimately, destructive behavior.

For instance, if he believes he is valuable based on performance, he is in for a rough ride and he'll take your daughter with him. He'll never be secure because none of us ever stop performing. If he believes he gets his affirmation from the culture's definition of success, he won't listen to God or his wife. If he believes he deserves punishment because of failure, he will struggle with depression, shame, and condemnation. If he can only be secure when he's in total control, he will be an insecure tyrant.

And whatever he believes, he'll lead his wife and children into the same attitudes. Belief systems deserve close scrutiny and must be adjusted to align with the truth according to Jesus, the Word of God.

Where the man leads, the family follows.

However, it's not enough to know "truth" in one's head. You must live according to the truth. James 4:17 says that the one who knows what he should do and does not do it sins. It must be in the core of one's being. This doesn't come from being raised in a Christian home, being nice, being a good person, having a strong work ethic and a promising career, coming from a family of privilege, or being "quality marriage material."

This only happens when a person is born of the Spirit of God. Then we have the same Spirit—the Spirit who was active in original creation and who inspired the writing of scripture and who raised Jesus from the dead—living inside us.

This kind of man follows God more than his feelings. His word means something. What he believes in his heart, he knows in his head, he speaks with his words, and he demonstrates with his actions. He is a man of integrity.

It's a total package. If you don't have them all, then it's only a matter of time before the cracks in the foundation bring the whole house crashing down.

3) Grateful for his story

Next, this suitor should be grateful for what he has and constantly aware of the grace of God. He must avoid comparing himself with others and coveting what he does not have. This characteristic is a rare commodity in our world where fulfillment and thanksgiving remain elusive. This attitude of gratitude makes for a good steward. Recognizing we are responsible for what we are given develops character. If we don't use what we have, we lose it.

Too many young men are fixated on what they don't have. They're convinced that life is not fair, that they have not yet received what they deserve, as they complain about the injustice they received compared with others.

The reality is, none of us controlled when and where we were born or many of the circumstances surrounding our story. Life can be difficult. It's *not* fair. Injustices happen. People hurt us either intentionally or unintentionally.

But the good news of the gospel of Jesus Christ is that He has faced injustice, forever paid the debt of sin, and defeated the sting of death. Having been raised from the dead He now gives the same Spirit that raised Him to all those who believe. So we are no longer victims of life. We have the opportunity to be victors in life.

Excuses for anger, bitterness, addictions, fear, and prejudice are just symptoms of one who has avoided the cross experience. There is nothing wrong with us that dying wouldn't fix. If we were dead, our dysfunction would not be a problem.

Jesus made it possible for us to share in His death AND to experience the newness of the overcoming life through His miraculous work in redemption. Because He suffered in every way, we can overcome in *all* things.

This young man may have embraced a vicious lie that's popular in a lot of preschools and kindergartens: You can be anything you choose.

Although presented as an inspirational promise of possibility, this attitude actually creates a prison of confusion. While this sentiment may be well-meaning, the truth is you *can't* be anything you choose.

There are lots of things that you will never be. No matter how bad you want it, you can't be the President of the World, a bald eagle, or Superman. I would have chosen to be a great musician, but I don't have the ear. I would have chosen to be a great NBA star, but my height and coordination would not allow.

This simple, little lie creates too many choices. Without direction and definition, all we're left with is disillusionment. If you were dropped in the ocean with no land in sight and told you could swim in any direction you wanted, would you feel free? Personally, I would like to know which direction would get me closer to land.

Here's a much better promise: You can be exactly who God created you to be, and there's nothing else that could possibly be more fulfilling. And God Himself will guide you through the process, giving you clues and direction along the way.

Another common lie revolves around his circumstances or environment. He might have grown up believing that his "lot" is less or better than others. Either he'll be filled with pride thinking he's better than everyone else or he'll wrestle with rejection due to his apparent insignificance.

What he won't be is *grateful*. And that will keep him from being confident with the extent of his appointed sphere of influence. Note the testimony of the Psalmist:

> The Lord is my chosen portion and my cup;
> you hold my lot. The lines have fallen for me
> in pleasant places; indeed, I have a beautiful
> inheritance (Psalm 16:5-6).

A true sense of significance comes from taking what has been given and using it for the best possible results.

My earthly father is my hero. He had a ninth grade education. He and my mother reared five children on a

160 acre farm that he *bought* from his father. His two sons are in the ecclesial ministry, and all of their children are effectively fulfilling their equally important callings. His three daughters all have significant roles in their fields of ministry, having reared five devoutly Christian, culture-changing granddaughters.

He was the most grateful man I have known. In his later years after Mom died, we would sit under the big water oak in his front yard, with him chewing his favorite Red Man tobacco. I tried to join him, but I never acquired the taste. I wondered if I was too wimpy.

His old farm pickup truck had many miles and dents. He still used it all the time, but he had the money to buy a new one.

"Dad, why don't we get you a new truck?"

"Nah," he said. "What I've got is OK."

I wanted to bless him. I wanted to get something for him that he wouldn't get for himself. I kept trying.

"Well, you really like watching sports on TV. Why don't we get you a new and bigger TV?" I suggested.

"Nah," he said again. "The one I have will do."

I couldn't figure it out. So I asked him one day. "Dad, how did you become so content with your life?"

"Oh, I just decided to like what I have rather than want what I don't have."

That simple, wise advice would save a lot of men serious heartache.

4) Devoted as a disciple of Jesus

Fourthly, the man I want to marry my daughter must be a disciple of Jesus Christ.

Let's face it. What I have described above is a pretty high standard. None of us fully fit that bill. The only way any man could come close to meeting these four requirements is through the power of discipleship. We'll never get there in our own strength. Only Jesus can make us that kind of man.

God gave Adam a wife to help him in the work that God gave him. If a man doesn't know what God's called him to do, then why would he need a helpmate? He should be in the world, not of it, a prophet for change not a product of culture.

I'm not looking for a perfect man, but I am looking for a man who is committed to God's process. We're all on a lifelong journey to follow the great Master Jesus who shows us what it means to be a real man. I'm praying for a man who enjoys the journey, bears good fruit, and gives life to others.

And I'm looking for the guy who is intentional about knowing who he really is, doing what he says, using what he has, and following Jesus with passion.

By the way, my daughter asked if we could include an application.

FOR FURTHER STUDY

1. How can you tell when a man is secure in his identity
in Christ? Give a specific example.

2. What is the difference between a man who is solid in
his integrity and one who is not?

3. What one thing keeps you from being grateful? When
was the last time you stopped and considered all the ways
God has blessed you? Who did you tell?

4. Would you call yourself a devoted disciple of Jesus?
What fruit in your life backs this up?

5. When did you know for sure that you had transitioned
from being a boy to becoming a man? How would you help
a male who was never told by fathers that he is a man?

CHAPTER
MEN AND THEIR BIBLES
FOUR

God has revealed Himself throughout history, and the Bible is the record of that revelation. Without it we are left ignorant of the correct perspective on history and its purpose.

We can certainly understand, then, why a devilish scheme would be concocted to separate men from a proper understanding of the Scriptures.

If men who are comfortable in their skin as warriors truly discover the crime that has been committed they will rise up with a vengeance. Somebody needs to tell them:

The Bible has been stolen! The thief is not the communist we feared during the cold war or the terrorist who wages jihad in service of Allah. We would fight against that kind of obvious all-out assault.

But the heist happened so slowly under our noses that we didn't even notice the Bible is missing. After all, we still have lots of copies of Scripture lying around. In fact, the Bible still tops the best-seller lists and remains far and away the best-selling book of all time. Nothing is even close.

But less than 8% of American schools offer a Bible class, making the narrative of the Bible increasingly unfamiliar to the average student. And when it is mentioned, it's not given the respect and reverence that it deserves.

No other book has undergone attacks, criticism, and scrutiny like the Bible. For hundreds of years, scientists, philosophers, professors, and angry authors have argued that

Scripture can't be trusted, that it's filled with contradictions, and that it's an unreliable account.

The bottom line is that people who are upset with the Bible are really upset with Jesus.

The evidence that supports the credibility of the Bible as we read it today is overwhelming. So much so, we could write an entire book describing the merits of Christian Scripture.

We could marvel at how it was put together with so many different authors over such a long period of time while all retaining a common theme and fulfilling a common purpose.

We could argue that there are an incomparable number of ancient manuscripts that support its consistency as historically true.

We could show how it has been miraculously preserved.

We could demonstrate how the Scriptures challenge mankind in every way, calling us to a devoted life lived for God that cost many of the earliest Christians their lives.

We could bring evidence of its unique transformational influence in societies all over the world for thousands of years.

But the primary authority of the Scriptures comes from its relationship to the living Word of God: Jesus.

We learn from reading the Bible that Jesus is the agent of creation. He is the Word that brought creation into existence.

He is the sustainer of creation. He is the redeemer of creation. And He is the culmination of creation. Since history is about Him, and the Bible is recorded history, the Bible is about Him.

Ultimately, we can safely say that the reason the Bible is authoritative is because it is a trustworthy witness of the Living Word Himself, King Jesus.

Of course if one denies Jesus, if one chooses to rebel against God, they are free to argue that the Bible has no authority or relevance for their life.

But that choice doesn't make God's Word any less true.

Despite the fact that we can trust the reliability of Scripture, some argue that these antiquated stories written thousands of years ago don't have any bearing on our 21st Century world. This idea is both arrogant and misguided.

First, the Bible gives us the big picture of God's purpose in history from His divine perspective. God's redemption story has been going on since the Garden of Eden, it culminates in the Christ-event and continues in the story of each of our lives. God has told us the meaning of history so that we are not left to interpret events from our limited perspective. He didn't leave us at the mercy of historicists who revise history to conform to their humanistic worldview.

Second, the Bible gives us the knowledge of Christ that we desperately need as we develop an intimate relationship with Him. He is alive, and we can know Him. But He was a genuine historical figure; the Christ we know in the spirit is the same as the one revealed in the Scriptures that physically lived on earth 2,000 years ago.

Third, the Scriptures record the instructions given by Jesus and the early apostles we need to live this new kind of existence: eternal life. We have the Holy Spirit living in us, guiding us, and leading us into all truth found in Scripture.

We'll never know how to follow Christ, how to obey God, how to lead our families, or how to be real men if we don't know God's Word.

If the enemy can't get rid of the Bible, he'll do everything he can to twist it. Over time, we have become the victims of an insidious and effective scheme to steal the message by giving speckled spectacles to those who read it regularly. We've been manipulated to misread what's there and to read in things that aren't there.

As a result, it's really the *message* that's missing.

Of course this dilemma is not new. Jesus indicted the Pharisees of New Testament times for misreading, misunderstanding, and misinterpreting Scripture. *"You search the Scriptures because you think that in them you have eternal life; and it is they that bear witness about me"* (John 5:39).

They missed the *message*.

They were so concerned with "the jots and tittles" that they totally missed the main point of the Bible . . . Jesus.

The entire Bible, from Genesis to Revelation, from the Old Testament to the New, is about Jesus.

The Pharisees, chief priests, and Sadducees interpreted the Bible through a narrow, literal perspective. They expected all the promises and prophecies to be fulfilled exactly like the original hearers expected. They were looking for the physical restoration of Israel, the temple, the king, and the public humiliation of those who oppressed them.

All of that happened right in front of their eyes through Jesus, but not in the way they expected.

They missed the *message*.

The New Testament reveals that God had in mind more than the original hearers could imagine, but the fulfillment would be consistent to the transcendent, over-arching theme of Scripture.

 For instance the "seed" that God promised to Abraham turned out to be more than Isaac. Jesus, the ultimate Seed of Abraham, was able to fulfill the complete task of blessing the nations.

They missed the supernatural restoration that happened in their midst by rejecting the ultimate representative of mankind and Israel. In rejecting and mocking the resurrection, they sealed the fate of their blindness, while demanding that God be faithful to *their* version of His promise.

All of us face this same challenge. We must be careful not to demand that God be faithful to *our version* of His promise.

The new reality Jesus came to bring started with a miraculous life, a sacrificial death, a powerful resurrection, a glorious ascension, and the gracious gift of the Holy Spirit living in His believers.

In time this victory would affect every culture of the earth and thereby bring the blessings of Abraham's seed to the nations.

The apostle Paul writes to Timothy about the place of Scripture in his life and ministry.

> But as for you, continue in what you have learned and have firmly believed, knowing from whom you learned it and how from childhood you have been acquainted with the sacred writings, which are able to make you wise for salvation through faith in Christ Jesus. All Scripture is breathed out by God and profitable for teaching, for reproof, for correction, and for training in righteousness, that the man of God may be competent, equipped for every good work (2 Timothy 3:14-17).

He makes the point that, properly embraced, the Scriptures produce a man or woman fully equipped and competent for every good work. But a survey of Bible readers reveals something much different.

Only a small percentage of faithful Bible readers engage in good works for the glory of God.

Some polls reveal that Christians give less than 3% of their income to any kind of charitable cause.

The divorce rate among Christians is HIGHER than it is among non-Christians.

Christians have a lifestyle of confusion not much different from those who don't believe and don't read the Bible.

So in the midst of all the ministry conferences promising power and prophetic revelation, in the flood of books and blogs assuring us that the relevance of Scripture can be seen in the fulfillment of prophecy happening in the Middle East; under the deluge of TV preachers parading questionable interpretations of Scripture to tantalize the American consumer fixated with health, wealth, and stealth, we can hear the faint but ascending cry from the some men awakening from passive slumber: "I WANT MY BIBLE BACK!"

There are several misconceptions of Scripture that rob the true message from us.

The Bible is "a good luck charm." That is, a copy of the Bible itself is somehow endowed with divine power and can protect or give good luck to those who have it in the house, on the dashboard, or in their pocket. Stories are told of soldiers whose lives were saved by a bullet hitting the copy of the New Testament in their pocket. This has led some to treat it like a holy rabbit's foot.

The Bible is a book of moral stories and teachings to help us live a good life. Interestingly, we have to pick and choose which stories we want to read for this purpose, for the Bible tells of actions we don't really condone in our "moral" society. We learn of courage when we read of David killing Goliath. We learn of faith when we read of Abraham's journey. We learn of endurance when we read of Joseph or Job.

But if we didn't already have a definition of those virtues before we read, how would we know to pick those stories? There are also stories of incest, murder, lying, stealing—all by main characters in the story. The Bible is not a sanctified "Aesop's Fables." It is not to be grouped with other ancient collections of moral codes and mythical stories.

The Bible is like an owner's manual. Recently, a TV preacher made this exact point by stating, "When we got our refrigerator, we got an owner's manual. When we received Christ, we got another owner's manual, and it is the Bible." That leads to viewing the whole Bible as instructions, a rule book, or *The Spiritual Life for Dummies*.

When we have a problem, we turn to the problem solving section and read it like it was written for that problem. Some churches have even refused to produce a legal document of bylaws by stating that the Bible is their constitution and bylaws.

This view of Scripture seldom makes a healthy connection of the Old and New Testaments. The Bible becomes a set of moral instructions for daily living, like food laws, codes for sexual morality, or clothing instructions for priests.

This forces us to pick and choose which passages seem to fit, and the inapplicability of some sections allows us to discredit the portions that we don't like.

The truth is that there
is a progression from Old to New that must be recognized
before meaningful illumination is possible. This allows us to
understand the relevance that
can be found in ALL of God's Word.

The Bible is a compilation of random predictions, some already fulfilled and some yet to come. This approach appeals to human curiosity, conspiracy theories, secret messages and as a result, unwarranted popularity for lots of crazy books.

It suggests that current newspaper headlines are fulfilling specific prophecies, especially in the Middle East. With baited breath, people await another "prophetic" explanation of decisions made by political leaders of various countries. Historical events of the last century are granted the same dignity of New Testament scriptures as they are hailed as being fulfilled Old Testament scriptures. This approach can easily lead to our reducing the Scriptures to writings like *The Bible Code* or those written by Nostradamus and Edgar Cayce.

The Bible is primarily about Israel. This approach arises from the rigidly literal approach to interpretation that makes the Old Testament superior and the guide for understanding the New Testament. References to Israel and its future are kept literal and physical.

Since Israel as known in the Old Testament is not around any more, there is much speculation about the nature of today's Israel and what will happen in the future to produce another biblical Israel. For some, one's attitude toward modern Israel determines favor with God. The church is a parenthesis in time as we wait for the moment when the "prophecy clock" starts again. What *starts* that clock is up for much debate and makes for lots of speculative books and TV programs.

This approach essentially takes the Bible out of the hands of the ordinary believer. You have to be trained by prophecy experts to accurately understand any passage. The average Bible reader would not likely come to these conclusions.

This takes the focus off Jesus, His church, and making disciples and gives great emphasis to what is happening in the Middle East. If the church of Jesus Christ is not the central expression of His kingdom on earth, and is in fact just a parenthesis in history, then its importance is diminished and its success is doubted. The church has been taken out of its role of influence and reduced its value to "spiritual matters" and helping the poor. Essentially, the church has nothing to offer the arenas of business, politics, education, and the economy.

The Bible was written to me. This is sometimes called "illuminism." Every book, chapter, verse, and promise is read as if it was intended for the reader directly.

Passages can be taken out of context because the Spirit gives them personal meaning. The Old and New Testament divisions don't make much difference. It is just a matter of reading words and hearing the application for the reader at the time.

Of course, every verse in the Bible has relevance

and meaning for me, but that's not the same thing as suggesting it was written *to or about me*. I'm not the main character, the subject of Scripture. The Holy Spirit used human instruments in historical settings to convey the words of God for an intended meaning, and we are responsible to take that into account when we apply those meanings to our own lives.

So how *do* we approach the Bible? Paul indicates to Timothy that the goal of all Scripture was faith in Jesus the Christ. The whole book of Hebrews illustrates that He is the only mediator between God and man. That includes His unique role as the interpreter of the Scriptures that God has inspired and preserved for us. Since He is the goal and the subject of all God's purposes on earth, the correct lens through which we interpret Scripture is Jesus the Christ.

A priority for Jesus after His resurrection was to explain the Old Testament scriptures to His disciples (Luke 24:25). He explained it to them from a Christocentric perspective. These Jewish men, who were familiar with the expectations of Jewish leaders regarding the purposes of God, were rebuked for not understanding the prophecies that referred to Him and His necessary suffering.

But they were extremely energized by the full revelation they received from Jesus. They remarked to one another, *"Did not our hearts burn within us . . . while he opened to us the Scriptures?"* (Luke 24:32).

The Scriptures give an account of history from the perspective of God's purposes. As we know, history is not self-evident. It needs to be interpreted. The Bible gives us the grid to understand what has happened and what it means. Since God's purposes always lead to magnifying the Son, each historical event recorded in the Bible points toward Jesus.

In Abraham, Jesus is "the seed" that will ultimately bring blessings where Adam's sin brought curses.

In Israel, Jesus is the ultimate Son of God through whom He will do His final work.

In David, Jesus is the King who will reign over God's kingdom on earth.

In Solomon, Jesus is the wisdom of God for all the people of God.

In the prophets, Jesus is the restoration of His people.

In Matthew, Jesus is the fulfillment of Old Testament promise.

In Mark, Jesus is the present King who leads the world into His glorious kingdom.

In Luke, Jesus is the Servant who will save creation.

In John, Jesus is the first and final Word of God.

When we read God's Word through this lens, the impact is undeniable.

The New Testament completes and explains the Old

Testament. What was anticipated in the Old is embraced

in the New. "The age to come" has come through Jesus, and we can experience His eternal life right now in this life.

The new creation has begun. Sin has been forgiven fully in the final sacrifice of the Lamb of God. Believers have been regenerated through the same Spirit that raised Jesus from the dead. The love of God has been poured into the heart of every believer, and they are free from the obligation to live the self-centered life of flesh.

The Law has been fulfilled, and the Spirit who lives within produces what the law promised but could not produce. All bondage produced by sin is subject to the liberation of the Spirit as the power of the resurrection is released. Reconciliation to God is accomplished, and now we can get back to the original task of subduing the earth under His rule. We as new creations have the same future as Christ. Since we are in Him, His life is ours.

So how would a man who is eager to encounter Jesus through Scripture approach a biblical text? The obvious and simple answer is two-fold.

First, how does that text relate to Jesus, the subject of all text? Secondly, how do I relate to Jesus based on that text?

If it is an Old Testament promise and Jesus fulfills it, then I can expect certain blessings based on my relationship with Him. If it is a command, I can see where Jesus obeyed it and transferred the benefits to us, enabling me to do the same. If it is a narrative, I can see the climax being in Jesus and

its affects on my life. If it is a prophecy, I can see when and how Jesus fulfills it and if that affects me.
When we truly embrace the Scriptures properly we will be transformed every time we read God's Word. We'll be more motivated to tell those we love about the good news of what God has done in Jesus.

We will stand boldly with those who are tired of being robbed and cry, "I want my Bible back."

To the superstitious we say, "I want my Bible back."

To the moralist, "I want my Bible back."

To the legalist, "I want my Bible back."

To the mystic, "I want my Bible back."

To the literalist, "I want my Bible back."

To the narcissist, "I want my Bible back."

We are hungry for the bread of heaven, thirsty for the water of life, longing for the purpose of history. We refuse to reduce life to regulations. We abhor manipulative attempts to control our time, capture our money, and capitalize on our curiosity.

We are tired of feeling ill equipped to live and minister like Paul and Peter. Paul said we could be fully equipped, and we want it. Peter told Jesus that no one else had "the words of life."

Those who have stolen the tool of the Spirit can't keep it any longer. We want our Bible back. We want to spend our lives with those who are devoted to Jesus, and we will not settle for survival when victory is available. We are on a pilgrimage, but not to some Zion of history past. We are on a trek to discover and then declare the glories of the Son for whom the world was created.

It is our God-given privilege to know the Son, and we are not comfortable with others telling us what He said when we can hear it ourselves.

We will find our spiritual hunger satisfied when we again value the Holy Scriptures as God does.

We are men of the Bible, and we can't be comfortable in our skin without God's Word.

1. What is the promise related to properly interpreting the Scripture? (2 Timothy 3:14-16)

2. What specific benefit have you experienced through your personal study of Scripture? What else are you hoping to receive from your daily devotions?

3. What specific thing prevents you from regularly reading your Bible? What can you do about it?

4. How could your small group leader, accountability partner, or church leader help you in this challenge?

CHAPTER
MEN AND THEIR FAILURES
FIVE

It was a shot to my gut that literally took my breath away.

This blow was not struck with a fist, a foot, a blade, or a bullet. I was leveled by crushing words.

Our son had come home from college to tell his mom, his sister, and me that he no longer believed what the rest of the family held so deeply. Furthermore, he had no intention of living with the values we held and he had followed up to that point. He let us know that he was going to lead a life contrary to ours which would mean he wouldn't be around much.

We heard it directly from him. In the future, our fellowship with the family would rarely include my first-born son.

We were all devastated.

How could this happen? What did we do wrong?

He graduated from a fine Christian high school and arrived at college as an honor student and a committed Christian. Just four years later he was renouncing what he described as "narrow minded Christian values," so he could be free to existentially experience all that life had to offer. "Higher learning" had led him to realize the Christian morality of his youth was a naïve and confining restraint that prevented him from experiencing "real life."

As I sat there stunned listening to these terrifying words, a rush of emotions instantly hit me. Guilt, condemnation, fear, hopelessness, and shame flooded my heart and my mind.

Since then I've met thousands of parents, grandparents, siblings, and friends who have shared this horrendous ordeal. All of us were devastated by the estrangement of someone we love deeply.

This kind of depression is also common to other crises in our lives. Betrayal, divorce, being fired from a job, financial collapse, contracting a serious disease, and many other jarring events become unbearable weights on our shoulders. Just waking up and facing a new day becomes a life and death struggle.

But every parent who has watched their son or daughter suffer knows a deeper level of pain. This becomes even more agonizing when the circumstances are the result of your child's sinful and self-destructive choices.

Whether you've yet to face this kind of storm, you're in the middle of them, or maybe even between storms, all of us face these kinds of life-altering situations. When you find yourself here, there's only one thing on your mind: Is there a way out of this? And if so, where is my help going to come from?

It's easy to feel like no one has ever gone through what we're experiencing, but that's not true. In Scripture we see that King David knew the pain of having a son go astray. Absalom turned against his father and his God. He began to live a lifestyle to spite his father and ultimately intended to dethrone him. David agonized over this. He lost sleep. He got sick. He cried out to God.

Most of us remember all the great things that God did in his life, but David was no stranger to tough times. I'm glad he shared them with us so honestly. His confessionals have helped me. It is probable that Psalms 42 and 43 were written by his companions during this time and are valid expressions of his pain.

His enemies both internal and external were attacking him from every vantage point. When someone as important as your child is estranged, every weight seems heavier and every obstacle seems more difficult. Life seems too hard to endure. There was more than enough responsibility and pressure for the king of Israel to live in a state of constant stress and anxiety. The bitter pain of a wayward son by itself is enough to keep you up at night. Both of these together had to create extra weight on his heart, complicating every decision he made.

Joy was a distant memory, and a way out of the crisis felt impossible. If you've never had a child break your heart, you may still identify with this kind of pain if you've been betrayed by someone you've loved completely.

When our world is shaken, we often feel that we are abandoned by God. The comfortable place of fellowship and peace we've enjoyed in private and corporate worship is gone. The pain has pushed out God, and we wonder if He is going to fight to have us back or just leave us there.

Of course we know in our minds that God has not left us, but sometimes it sure feels like it in our hearts. If He is not absent, at the very least He's different. It doesn't feel the same, and we want the old feeling back. It's been so long, we forget what it feels like to laugh and enjoy life. We wonder if it's even possible to find joy and happiness.

Back when we were enjoying life, we didn't know this tragic event was in our future. If we had known then, we would not have enjoyed those moments of fun and celebration. The guilty thought wanders through our mind—"Maybe if I had been praying seriously instead of enjoying a light moment this would not have happened."

Our soul screams, "This hurts SO BAD, this pain is so intense, I'll never enjoy life again!"

I wonder. Is it possible to find something through our pain that is more valuable than comfort? Could it be that God moves us from those comfortable places of fellowship to introduce us to greater levels of grace? Is there a different aspect of His character we could never know during what we would call "the good times"?

I have known people who had a depth in their relationship with God that they could not articulate. In their suffering they found something more precious than riches and luxury.

They met God in a supernatural way in the unplanned place of pain.

There will never be a shortage of critics and nay-sayers. They're always around. Some of them whisper in our minds while others discourage us at the office and even in our homes. Wherever they are, the one constant is that the weight of their words are heavy. Their voices are loud in a manner that transcends volume.

Internal accusation has as much effect on us as external. We know people were accusing David of trusting in a defective God, but I'm sure David was hearing the whispers in the supernatural realm too. It's no different for us today.

These mocking accusations always attack the ability and intentions of God. We're persuaded that either He can and He won't or He can't no matter how much He wants. In that moment, all the creeds we have recited and the scriptures we have previously quoted are put to the test.

It is easy to sing about and pray to a sovereign God when Absalom is with you in worship. But what happens when the whole plan of a healthy family serving God together goes out the window?

And when your plans go out the window, you begin to wrestle with all kinds of dark thoughts.

"Maybe all that talk about how prayer changes things is all wrong."

"Maybe prayer is just for fine tuning the one praying."

"Maybe the universe is set up to run on laws and principles, and God does not interrupt it. Absalom has his own free will doesn't he? Maybe God can't or won't violate that by influencing him. Would that be unfair and contrary to His ways?"

"Maybe prayer is just something we came up with because we need to believe in something."

"Have I lost my faith? Have I been deceived all this time?"

"Is all this 'trusting God' stuff a cruel joke?"

If you have ever experienced crisis in your soul, you recognize the questions.

The opinions of other people are never as painful as your own thoughts and the drifting attitudes of your emotions. When there's nothing for us to fight, we turn on ourselves and start pounding away. When our soul is dry we feel all alone, we feel like failures, we feel hopeless and worthy of being punished.

David compares it to being pounded by wave after wave of the surf. After already being driven into the ocean floor by a heavy wave, another comes along just as you raise your head and dare to hope. Then down you go again, with another crushing blow, taking the breath away and dashing what remains of an already weak faith. The nights seem to last forever, and the days go by like a meaningless blur.

It shouldn't surprise us that this exact technique is one of the most difficult training exercises for Navy SEALS. The physical toll is great, but the emotional damage is unbearable.

Memory becomes a powerful weapon in the hands of the voice of accusation. They pound away like the crashing surf that erodes mountains of rock.

"Remember when you chose not to spend time with your son?"

"Remember when you corrected him in anger?"

"Remember when you forced your values upon him because he didn't agree with you?"

"Remember when you didn't pray because you were watching sports?"

"Remember that vacation when you became so irritated you lashed out in anger?"

And once these memories have taken their toll, accusation moves in for the kill. It won't stop until you admit it's all your fault.

"You did this. You wounded his soul, and now this is the result. What about your sin that still owns you? Cheating, lying, selfishness, the shame of your youth, rebellion toward your own parents . . . remember those?"

From his honest agony in Psalms we realize that David faced all of these thoughts during his life, yet God still included these words in His inspired and perfect Word for our benefit.

Wrestling with accusation doesn't make you a failure; giving up the fight does.

You give up the fight when you stop wrestling and start repeating. It sounds something like this.

"Yeah, where is my God when I need Him? Has He forgotten me? If He had known this was going to happen, why didn't He just prevent me from having children? It would be better for Absalom if he had never been born than to deny God and bring shame on the body of Christ and our family — and me. What kind of weak father must I be to have a son turn from my teachings? I have no business representing God in any way."

As tempting as it is to entertain and embrace these thoughts, we must refuse. Despite what our feelings tell us, we're not the only ones who have felt this way. In fact, we're in good company.

Abraham. Noah. Moses. Gideon. Jonah. Jeremiah. And of course, David.

Remember, King David is a forerunner to our ultimate ruler, King Jesus. I wonder if Jesus ever felt this kind of depressing sorrow. The fact that Jesus' relationship with the Father gave Him insight into God's plan did not prevent Him from experiencing the full weight of human emotion. He was engaged, not distant. He felt the sting of disappointment, mistrust, and of course, betrayal.

He cried with Mary and Martha when Lazarus died. He endured the torment of Judas' betrayal. He knew the disappointment of being abandoned in the hour of His greatest crisis. He was mocked and publicly shamed to a degree that we cannot understand.

If all of that was not enough, what about when He was on the cross and felt the abandonment of His Father? I can't really imagine that. How could God abandon God? That is too much for me. He survived the garden and the grave. But even the biblical scholars don't know how to explain the Trinity. He was God-Man. I am just a man.

Like Jesus, David wrestled, but he refused to quit fighting. He lectured his soul. Why should we accept the verdict of our own limited perspective? I see and hear and feel, and my soul forms my reality based on this data. But David discovered a higher reality that was more trustworthy than the version offered by his own soul.

Memory doesn't have to be unkind. We can choose to prioritize God's redemptive power over our mistakes. It only happens when we're proactive and intentional. We must not follow the whims of our soul; instead we must lead them in following God's truth.

> Why are you cast down, O my soul,
> and why are you in turmoil within me?
> Hope in God; for I shall again praise him,
> my salvation and my God.
>
> My soul is cast down within me;
> therefore I remember you
> from the land of Jordan and of Hermon,
> from Mount Mizar (Psalm 42:5-6).

If our focus is on our actions, we will either be accused or arrogant. But if our focus is on His works, hope arises over the horizon of a barren and bleached soul. "THEREFORE I REMEMBER" is a choice. We have the camera of memory in our hands. We can focus on our mess-ups or on His fix-ups.

David had a history with God. Long before David came on the scene God had been working with His people, weaving their journey of redemption and hope for all mankind. His story took place in the context of God's larger plan for all people.

He knew of the covenant God had made with his forefather Abraham and had a record of God's faithfulness through the ages. He knew by heart the story of the Exodus when God miraculously delivered His people to the very land David was living in. He was keenly aware of the covenant God had made with Moses and had seen God's faithfulness to keep it. He knew the story of the miraculous deliverances of the various judges who saved Israel time after time.

His life was a piece of a larger puzzle, another chapter in God's over-arching story of all mankind. He could remember the day Samuel came out to his father's house to pick God's king. He could still feel the excitement as he unexpectedly came home and was anointed to be that king.

Nevertheless, his knowledge wasn't stronger than the emotional power of his soul. Left to his feelings he would have been stuck in a pit of despair.

God hasn't changed. He will never abandon His purpose or the people who love and obey Him. He has proven time and again that He can work through the various decisions men have made and still bring His plan together on time.

He took Adam's sin and made it an opportunity to show His mercy. He took Abraham's faithlessness to reveal His faithfulness. He took Jacob's manipulation to reveal His

sovereign grace. He took Israel's desire for a king to show
His kingship. He cannot be thwarted by man's choices . . .
ever . . . not David's or Absalom's, not yours, and not mine.

We have a history with God that's even better than David's.
He was living in the preparatory stage of history. We live
in the culmination stage. His hope was directed toward
the chapters of God's progressive revelation in history.

Our history includes David's but continues on. After
David and his son, Solomon, Israel fell into apostasy again,
but God was faithful to His covenant. They lost their land
and their status as a sovereign nation. They were exiles in
Babylon, but God did not forget or abandon His plan. He
called and sent prophets to encourage them that one day
God would deliver them and restore His original purpose
on earth. There would be a day of the Lord to vindicate
His people and purpose. It would make the day of evil's
seeming triumph retreat into its rightful place of defeat.

That day arrived with the birth of the promised Messiah;
Jesus truly is Immanuel, "God with us."

He arrived as the new beginning, the new Adam, the Seed of
Abraham, the greater Moses, the ultimate Israelite, the Son
of David, the ultimate Son of Man, and the Lamb who takes
away the sins of the world. He fulfilled the promises of the
Old Testament, inaugurated the New Covenant, proclaimed
freedom for the captive, established His people on earth, and
once and for all defeated the forces of sin, death, and hell.

He accomplished this through His atoning death, miraculous
resurrection, and glorious ascension. He then sent the Holy

Spirit to live in the new believers so they could get on with representing God on earth like the original plan for Adam and Eve called for.

We're not like David because we don't have to look to the future for hope; Jesus forever provided everything anyone could ever need for life and godliness.

I am sorry that many sincere Christians have not been taught to find this hope in God's Word.

They have seen the Bible as a collection of doctrines, promises to individuals, and moral lessons. Because they have not seen it as God's perspective on history with beginning and conclusion, they have missed the grand purpose of creation and the awesome beauty of redemption.

They have found that when their world falls apart, they have scant bits of scripture to hold on to, and those don't always suffice. The Bible is not a series of bullet points or spiritual sayings you'd find in a greeting card or a fortune cookie.

With a grasp of the big picture, we understand that all human history submits to a sovereign God who rules even when it doesn't appear that way. And those relentless waves of sorrow and remorse that all of us have experienced? They belong to God too.

When David remembered with the camera focused on God, he used the personal possessive pronoun. Those were "Your waterfalls," "Your breakers," "Your waves."

The devil is an instrument, a bit player in this drama confined by the limits of the role he's been given. He is never the original cause or the final word. He may stir up the sea, but only under God's sovereignty. I must settle things with God, and then under His direction I can resist the devil—as God shows me where and how.

Counsel for the soul is healthy. The internal conversation must come in line with reality as God defines it. Notice that in these two Psalms he repeats his lecture to his soul three times!

> Why are you cast down, O my soul,
> and why are you in turmoil within me?
> Hope in God; for I shall again praise him,
> my salvation and my God (Psalms 42:5-6,
> 42:11, 43:5).

There is reason for hope! God was faithful before your crisis, and when it's all over, He will again show Himself faithful. He has never given us any valid evidence that He is faulty in His promises. No one can accuse Him of breaking His promise or ignoring His commitment. Though His fulfillments may look different than we expected, He has come through on them all and even given us an explanation of its new form.

"This is really that . . ." is a common explanation for those who walk with Him.

I'm sure we can't imagine the fear the disciples had when they finally understood that He was leaving them. I would have panicked for sure. But He didn't leave them without hope. When He promised, "I'm sending" and "I'm coming," He gave them hope to go on even though things would be more difficult than they could have imagined.

It was a new day. No more long walking trips with Him and the others as they physically watched Him heal, deliver, feed, and teach. Now a new day was upon them, and they were terrified. How does one live when the most important person in their lives is away?

"I will send . . ." and "I will come . . ."

He told them that it was better for them if He went away. "If I don't go He, the comforter, will not be able to come." It is hard to believe that when your heart is heavy and you have no idea what it's supposed to look like.

The main thing we see in this encounter with Jesus and His disciples is that He cared for them and their fears. And He still cares today.

He cares for you and me.

He cares for parents who long for their children to be safe, healthy, and in a right relationship with their Creator.

What was the source of their hope? The answer is simple. It's the only real source of hope that any of us have. But it's deep enough, wide enough, and long enough to cover any challenge we'll ever encounter.

They trusted Jesus.

Before, they had Him physically. Now they would be closer to Him than ever, in a much different way. He would send the Holy Spirit to them to make all of them temples of the living God.

They had access to personal, private, and corporate fellowship with God through the indwelling Spirit. They were empowered from within to do things they had watched Him do. The task that seemed too large to even tackle was within reach. They could make disciples of all nations and get about bringing the redemption He had purchased to all creation.

And through the Spirit of God, we have that same access today.

But Jesus promised still more.

"I will come . . ."

Make no mistake, He will be back. Oh, He came in the person of the Holy Spirit to live in them. As if that was not enough, He will also be back to culminate things. It won't go on forever without His return. He is not coming back to do the job He gave disciples. He has given all that is needed for that.

He will come to be celebrated as the God who loved His creation enough to become incarnate Himself. He was resurrected bodily and will bring creation itself to its full restoration. The new earth and heavens will testify eternally to the majestic care of the God who chose to be a Shepherd to each and every one of His sheep.

My mom and dad were married 50 plus years before she died. We were all afraid that dad might not adjust because he was so dependent on her. He did just fine for many years. But he would tell me as we sat under the giant oak tree in the front yard, "Son, you have no idea how much I miss her." I could feel the pain oozing from his teary eyes and broken tone, and I could only imagine.

Recently my wife Betsy went off with two of her best friends for a "girl's vacation." I was left alone for a few days at the house. Someone asked me if I was lonely or sad. Actually, I enjoyed the solitude and freedom of my personal schedule. But then a strange thought hit me. If you've been married for any period of time and your wife has gone on a trip without you, I'm sure you've wondered the same thing.

"What if she were not coming back? What would I do without her?"

I thought of my dad and his loneliness. I would have a whole different viewpoint if she were not coming back.

Jesus is coming back, yet no one knows the day or the hour. It may be days, years, decades or even centuries. Where is the hope in that?

This truth means that every day is filled with meaning. Every choice has lasting consequences. It's not too late to change. God is in control and will have the last word. Everything He intended for the earth will be accomplished; righteousness will be ultimately rewarded, and wrong will be judged.

He has not abandoned His earth or the people who live on it. We are part of a long narrative and play a vital role in it. The story hasn't finished yet.

At the same time, the truth is He has already come. History is not a "lame duck" existence, where we all wait meaninglessly killing time until He returns. There is a mission He has given us that He expects to be completed. Jesus came to do on earth everything necessary for us to be delivered from the effects of sin's intrusion. He has come in the person of the Holy Spirit to comfort and equip us. He is more real to us than to the disciples who literally walked with Him in Judea.

He is ready to reveal Himself to us in every situation of life. There is so much more to know of Him. And every new aspect we discover frees us even more to be the image-bearers He created. He has proved through history that He will take every circumstance and weave it into a garment of praise. Over and over He has, and there is no reason to believe He will stop now.

At this point you may be asking, "So what am I supposed to do now?"

First, have a good talk with your soul. Tell the truth as God defines it. It's OK to vent your frustrations as David did. God can handle anger, fear, and frustration from us. He is not sensitive or insecure. He wants radical, courageous honesty. But don't stop there.

After you pour out your heart, address your own thinking, feeling, and choosing in your soul. Use David's words if it helps or write your own. It is no time to be worried about grammar or religious protocol. No one except you and God needs to know. Address the lies that scream in your ears.

God cares for you more than you can imagine. God can change any circumstance. There's no crisis, challenge or obstacle that He can't overcome. God is not afraid to influence our choices. In fact, if He didn't first convict us, none of us would have ever chosen to believe (John 6:44).

Prayer is His idea. He told us to pray and to expect to receive an answer (Matthew 7:7-11). Your children's choices are not your fault. God does not take blame for Adam's transgression. Neither does He consider Himself disqualified as a Father because He had children go astray.

God is not punishing you for your sins. He did that when He put your sins on Jesus. Don't be guilty of disregarding His sacrifice by punishing yourself when God has settled it at the cross.

Second, realize you will laugh again. In fact, laugh now by faith. Laugh because you trust God more than you fear your crisis or hurt from your pain. Abraham and Sarah named their son Isaac, which means "he laughs" because of what their lifelong challenge produced in their lives.

One of my best friends was pastor of a small Baptist church and was trying to bring some needed changes in its worship and strategies. While away on a week's vacation, he was contacted and told that he had been fired by the deacons. When I called him, we were crying over his pain and the disappointment in the situation as well as the overall pettiness of men.

I remember saying, "Do you remember when we were freshmen football players in college and one of the players died during practice?"

"Sure," he said. "And why would you want to bring that up now? We're sad enough."

"Well, remember how we sat around that night wondering if they would disband the team and suspend the athletic program because of the tragedy? Would we lose our scholarships and have to leave school? We were all offering our opinions of what would happen and making predictions. Then do you remember some years later when several of the team got together and were laughing about how scared we were? Well, do you think one day you and I will remember this day when you were fired unjustly and laugh about the comedy of errors that brought us here?"

"Yeah, I suppose."

"Then let's laugh by faith now." So we did.

The laugh may be forced for now, but it is a deposit of hope in God who will again cause you to praise Him. Joy is essential to healthy life. It is based not on circumstances but on the character of God. Remember, Paul rejoiced in prison. He also changed the Roman Empire by writing letters from his cell. He could somehow grasp a little of the reality that history is totally under God's control and therefore his part was not to criticize the script, but play the assigned role.

Third, get back to work. Your assignment is not suspended because of someone else's choice. Their choices do not control you. Yours do.

I am told that the families of addicts must make the hard choice to live their own lives, or eventually their lives fall apart too. It is not easy, but it is right to refuse to let your children's choices dictate your life. It doesn't mean you don't care. It means you care enough to turn them over to God.

Obey God's Word, faithfully embrace the responsibilities He's given you, and trust Him completely.

We as parents have difficulty in releasing children even when they are obviously old enough to make choices that have consequences we can't prevent.

Remember the father figure in the story of the man with two sons. The one we call "the prodigal" left his father rather unceremoniously and lived in hedonistic rebellion. I'm sure the father wept as he prayed for his wayward son, but he kept the farm going.

Because the father was faithful with his responsibilities, when the prodigal finally returned, there was a home to come back to. They had all the resources they needed to throw a massive party and invite everyone they knew to celebrate with them.

Even though the son was creating trouble for the entire family during his rebellion, his father pressed on. The joyful service of our lives may be the only hope the disobedient child ever sees.

Pray and obey. I know—you're already doing that. But don't underestimate its importance. God answers prayer. He sometimes purifies our petitions before He answers them.

Remember the man who wanted Jesus to cast demons from his convulsing son? "Jesus, if you can . . . deliver my son." Jesus' reply was to redirect his request. "It's not if I can, but if you can believe." "Then help my unbelief."

When you're desperate enough, you want your prayers to be refined if that means they'll be effective. We don't want to just throw up vain requests, but the key is to keep praying without worrying if we are praying properly. If our prayers need adjusting, God will do it. He knows what we need before we even ask.

> Send out your light and your truth;
> let them lead me;
> let them bring me to your holy hill
> and to your dwelling! (Psalm 43:3)

You need to expect God to intervene. That doesn't mean He needs you to tell Him how. Our need to fix and control sometimes bleeds over into our prayers. He is capable of creative ways of intervening. We ask, and then we listen and obey. He will lead you to pray appropriately. He really wants to share with us the partnership of bringing His kingdom to every situation on earth.

One day while I was praying for our son, I was led to pray for his friends and ask that one might speak the Word of God to him. I hesitated for a moment as I wondered if I was overstepping my bounds. I didn't want to tell God how to fix the situation, but this was the desperate plea of a loving father.

Later my son told me about one of his business associates who came to him during that time and said, "David, why don't you wake up and start acting like who you are? You're a conservative Christian who is trying to live like someone you're not. Go back to your roots." It was part of the process of restoration. God likes for us to participate with Him as He works through us.

Get your church to pray and stand with you in your crisis. Not everyone needs to know details, but our humility and their love make a good mix. We are so close to the situation, we need others with more objective perspectives to join us in the battle. Don't be too proud to ask for help.

In the midst of your own pain, look for opportunities to pray for others who are also experiencing a dry soul and its pain. Losing our lives for the sake of others is still the essence of God's life. They're out there, and you'll find them if you really look. Pray for them at least as much as you pray for your own situation.

Success in this process is not measured by the return of your wayward child. To make their return the epitome of your hope is to submit to a cruel idolatry. It is enough to embrace our Father who loves more than we can imagine and pray for the powers of darkness to be dispelled by the gracious revelation of the Spirit.

Getting what you're asking for is not the source of your hope. God alone is our source of salvation and the reason for our hope.

"Hope in God; for I shall again praise him, my salvation and my God" (Psalm 42:11). Notice it is God alone who is our salvation and God. We can't afford to make the answer to our prayer into a god that determines our joy. His truth and light will bring us to Him, and with His perspective we can rejoice.

While you're going through your crisis, the most important change is not in your circumstances; it will be in you.

Whatever God may be doing in your child, you are the one in pain, and God has something for you beyond taking away the pain. He does not delight in watching us squirm in our circumstances. He brings pain only when there is something greater for us to embrace. He is not willing that we live continually with such shallow values as ease and convenience.

The happiness of so many families is a façade; behind the smiling faces and small talk you find broken, hurting people. God wants your family to have a depth of substance, a strong foundation of intimate unity that's answered the challenge of crisis.

David was so paralyzed by the rebellion of Absalom that he almost lost his kingdom by grieving when Israel needed a king to lead them. As difficult as it must have been, he had to embrace his bigger assignment even when his soul was heavy and he wanted to throw in the towel. (Read the whole story in 2 Samuel 13-19.)

As men you and I have a responsibility to lead our families and to be leaders in the family of God. We have been baptized into the family of God and our covenantal ties are stronger than our blood ties. Of course this does not diminish our responsibilities in family. 1 Timothy 3:4-5 tells us that a man should faithfully lead his home before becoming an overseer in the house of God.

God is looking for real men who are comfortable in their own skin, willing to lead their families and to be leaders in the family of God.

These men aren't free from pain, but they're filled with a patient hope. They aren't overwhelmed by their souls. They're committed and obedient to God's plan.

Stay faithful to the responsibilities God's given you. Keep praying and looking down the road for the return of your wayward child.

You can be this kind of man. God hasn't called you to be anything else.

FOR FURTHER STUDY

1. What event in your life has impacted you like Absalom's rebellion affected David?

2. Have you been paralyzed by your failure or disappointment? What happened? How have you dealt with it?

3. Specifically describe a crisis that you led your family or the family of God through. What did you do well? What could you have done better?

CHAPTER
MEN AND THEIR WOUNDS
SIX

We are deeply flawed but unconditionally loved. We can acknowledge our failures, knowing they won't disqualify us for His love. It takes some time for this message to sink in, but in time, it will.

It's better to be forgiven than perfect. When we understand and receive God's unlimited forgiveness, we're set free from the fear of failure. And once we're free, we can face life with all its past pain and future challenges.

It's no secret that our culture is filled with people begging for purpose and significance. Some of the best-selling books of the last few years have addressed this theme. This hunger for meaning and importance transcends age, ethnicity, religion, and location.

Sociologists give different names to different generations—names like *Baby Boomers*, *Generation X*, and *Generation Y* or *Millenials*. They've grown up under different circum-stances, faced a variety of challenges, and developed certain values and characteristics. But the one thing that they all share is this sense of dissatisfaction in their search for purpose. No matter where you go, men want to know that they matter. They want their lives to count.

Deep down they wrestle with the fear that their lives will end up wasted.

In the last chapter, we looked at the effect of Absalom's disobedience on David. As we look deeper into the life of Absalom, we'll discover the tragedy that surrounds any man who wastes his life through failing to deal with pain. Absalom had great potential. He was the most handsome young man of the land. He was a king's son, and not just any king, but the greatest king to ever lead Israel. He could have had just about anything he wanted. His father's kingdom was large, and he was surely destined to rule somewhere.

An awful event became a turning point for him. His beautiful sister, Tamar, was raped by one of David's sons by another wife. Absalom's wicked half-brother, Amnon, was consumed with lust for Tamar that it made him physically sick. A manipulative friend of Amnon's developed a plan to take advantage of the young girl, to get her alone and defenseless. Despite her desperate pleas, Amnon raped her.

Later when King David heard of this despicable deed he was furious, but he did not execute Amnon because Amnon was his first born.

Absalom was filled with hate for Amnon and overwhelmed by the injustice and abuse his beloved sister had suffered. Refusing to confront his hurt or to allow Tamar to confront the situation, he allowed his resentment to direct his life. He could only think of how he would avenge this awful deed.

This incident was the beginning of his tragic end. He would never be the same again.

Two years later, when the opportunity came, he invited all of his brothers to a party. He ordered his men to kill Amnon once he had plenty of wine. His servants obeyed and murdered Amnon that very night.

Absalom hated Amnon and resented his father, the king, for the perceived injustice related to the event. When Amnon was murdered, Absalom fled the region and stayed in hiding for three years.

David's heart longed to be reconciled with his hurting son. He made overtures toward him when he was in hiding, inviting him back from exile to live in the land and to return home to be with his father. But Absalom would not come without a plan. He was afraid because he was too focused on the pain of personal injustice.

Eventually, when he did return from exile, Absalom would sit at the gates of Jerusalem and draw the hearts of the king's subjects to himself. He gave the rest of his brief and wasted life to rallying the people of Israel against his father, King David.

In the end, he led a subversive rebellion to overthrow the king and seize the thrown and was actually able to run his father and his closest supporters out of the city and across the Jordan River. As the battle continued, Absalom's massive hair was caught in the branch of a tree with him left dangling. David's army killed him there.

Absalom died hanging from a tree, which is a clear picture of being cursed. *"Cursed is everyone who is hanged on a tree"* (Galatians 3:13). But even worse is this telling verse:

> Now Absalom in his lifetime had taken and set up for himself the pillar that is in the King's Valley, for he said, "I have no son to keep my name in

remembrance." He called the pillar after his own name, and it is called Absalom's monument to this day (2 Samuel 18:18).

Earlier in the story we discover that Absalom did have three sons and a daughter (whose name was Tamar), but here we find that no son would be able to carry on his legacy. No one knows what happened to his children, but he did not recognize them as his legacy. He had to put his name on a monument in order to be remembered.

What a tragic, wasted life! All that potential—yet in the end, all that remained was a stone with his name on it and a tragic story of what might have been. Absalom's pain became the wound that never healed, the infection that led to his early death.

A life filled with talent, promise, and every opportunity drifted into oblivion memorialized by a lonely monument and a cautionary tale.

Objects don't make great monuments. Whether it's a building, a business, a ministry, or a grant, nothing lasts like the investments that we make in people. A son or daughter to carry on what really matters, what God has done in our lives, is worth more than any other monument.

It doesn't even have to be a biological child. After all, David made Mephibosheth his son even though he was the natural son of his best friend Jonathan. David wanted to invest in the son of his friend to honor the legacy and memory of Jonathan.

Absalom hadn't invested in anyone, so the only thing that would remember his time on earth was a monument and this sorrowful story.

What went wrong?

THE ANATOMY OF A WASTED LIFE

Absalom chose to harbor his hurt. When he saw his sister Tamar in pain, he wouldn't get help and healing or allow his sister to either. He chose to internalize and bury it deeper.

The wound got down to the core of his being and began to narrow his life's focus. He couldn't see except through the eyes of pain from his gaping wound. In fact, it was this wound that shaped his life rather than the purpose for which He was created.

Like any untreated wound, Absalom's "father-wound" got infected, and it defined him. His motto was something like, "My pain is your fault." Getting even was more important than getting well. He would not admit his hurt, and therefore it continued to do its destruction in the darkness of a closed soul.

One of the reasons I believe the Psalms are divinely placed in the Bible is the vulnerability of the psalmist. Several of them begin with confessions of pain and doubt, but end with triumph when a new perspective is granted (Psalm 73). But "the lament psalms" continue with the pain and close without a positive note (Psalm 88).

The fact that the hurt is exposed is instructive. If it's brought to the light, that may not mean the wound is fixed instantly, but once it's in the open the process of healing can begin. God's grace is so aggressive that often all that is needed is the admission of pain, and grace rushes in like light into a dark room when the window is open.

Absalom spends precious time scheming and planning to avenge his pain. He uses all his energy to dishonor his father and prove him wrong. And his subversion is not just against his father, but against the king.

Could it be that much of the irrational rebellion of some children is an attempt to dishonor the father or the King (God) whom they think caused their pain? They conclude that God could have stopped it and didn't. He must be somewhat to blame.

An old country preacher once said, "It won't do any good to preach the measles if you have the mumps. The congregation will all go to bed with the mumps." They catch what has caught us. Our verbal instructions won't make much difference.

I don't think it was an accident that Absalom died hanging from a tree. It was God's testimony of his life. Those who refuse grace have no other future.

Those who embrace grace will find someone else on the tree in their place.

THE EXAMPLE OF A LIFE WELL-LIVED

You may have never realized it, but there are many comparisons and contrasts to be made between Absalom and Jesus.

Both were sons of David. Both suffered injustice.

We've already looked at Absalom. Now let's look at Jesus.

Born of a virgin, He was called a bastard. He was rejected by His own people and even His own family. He was mocked because of His humble beginnings, and He died outside the city in the place of criminals. Isaiah prophesied that those who saw Him would "esteem him stricken of God." In other words, all those who saw Jesus crucified outside the gates of Jerusalem assumed He was being punished, for what He had done, either by God or the Romans. He was getting divine justice. He died in ignominy. No one without divine revelation understood what was really happening.

But Jesus revealed the meaningful life. His response to personal injustice gives us not only a model but a power to live beyond it. Rather than being defined by His wounds, He lived with a larger, God-given purpose that alone defined Him.

Absalom's wound killed him because it never healed. Jesus' wounds allow all of us to be healed.

At age 12, when His mother scolded Him for not keeping up with the caravan after the feast, Jesus replied, "Did you not

know that I would be about My father's business?" He
was living for one purpose alone: to honor His Father.

Maybe at this early age He didn't know everything that
He would have to do in life, but He did know one thing:
Life was about honoring His Father. Without that single
focus, life gets too complicated to figure out.

It doesn't really matter who you marry, where you live,
what you do as a vocation if you aren't living for the
purpose for which you were created: to honor your Father.

Jesus lived with divine perspective. Because He lived
to honor His Father, He trusted the sovereignty of God
working through each and every event in life. He believed
that nothing was random in God's world. He knew the
biblical perspective on history. God had used every choice
of every man and woman to bring His purpose to fruition
on time.

Though many tried, no one was able to distract or delay
His focus, His obedience, and the successful pursuit of God's
plan for His life. This perspective enabled Him to find God
in every circumstance and to receive the grace to do what
God called Him to do.

I have heard that the initiation rite for the Cherokee
warrior, which marked his acceptance as a man, concluded
with him sitting blindfolded on a stump alone all night. He
was well aware of the wild beasts and the ferocious elements
of nature. If he stayed there all night, he would be allowed
to enter the ranks of manhood.

At sunrise the blindfold would be lifted, and he would discover that his father had been silently beside him the whole time.

God doesn't have to shout to those with divine perspective to announce His presence. His promise is enough. His past performance is sufficient. The cross proves it, and the resurrection guarantees it.

Though they can't see Him, they know He's right there beside them.

Divine perspective is a gift only for those living for the purpose of honoring God. Those who choose a lesser purpose can't see what is right before their eyes. Blind to His sovereignty and goodness, they discuss the unknown and doubt the obvious.

Jesus had the power to do what He could see. He not only knew people needed to be forgiven, *He* could forgive. He lived His life by the same power that raised Him from the grave. It is the same power that came at Pentecost to indwell His followers.

We have been given everything we need to overcome the pain of any wound we suffer, to receive healing, and to continue to pursue God's purpose for our lives.

If we are in right relationship with God, it's impossible for us to waste our lives. But that's not all. He has given us the privilege of sharing in His legacy.

Jesus spent His life with the twelve. When He died, most

would have said His life was a tragedy. He died young with no wife or kids to carry on. Unlike Absalom, He did not even have His name on any monuments or buildings. In fact, one of the reasons He was crucified was His prediction that the temple in Jerusalem would be destroyed.

He even lost one of His twelve.

But those eleven turned into 3,000 and then into a movement that swept through the known world and continues today to infect every culture on the face of the earth. More people have lived and died for that name than any other name in history, and we're just getting started. As we live for the same purpose and enjoy the same perspective, we have the privilege of making disciples of Jesus. Their fruit goes to our account as well as His.

Why would you settle for monuments when you could have sons? There are thousands waiting for someone to father and mother them. They long for someone without a political agenda to care for them. It's not too late for any who are still alive.

Retirement can be better if lived for others. The prime years are not too full to include investing in the next generations. Even teenagers can start making decisions now that will positively affect the generation of their grandchildren.

Someone might ask, "What if Jesus comes back soon?" I can assure you He won't scold you for living to give your life away. He told us to do business until He returns.

But wasted time will lead to a wasted life.

Your life is too precious to live defined by pain, a wound, fear, doubt, or meaninglessness. Today is your moment of change. Address your pain. Forgive! Embrace your life and trust God's grace to fill this day and every other with His purpose.

The rest will take care of itself.

You were designed to live with purpose. Your wounds were not meant to define you but to refine you.

Invest in people. There are sons to be raised and released. Let's get after it.

With this perspective, we will be more comfortable in our skin.

FOR FURTHER STUDY

1. What wound has had the biggest impact on your life? Have you been healed, or is the wound infected?

2. Are there situations or people you totally avoid because you associate them with this past pain? Has bitterness, unforgiveness, or hate crept into your heart?

3. Have you wounded someone who's still hurting and being defined by their pain? What do you need to do to make it right?

4. What is God's purpose for your life? Do you have the divine perspective to see God's sovereignty in what you're going through? Explain.

CHAPTER
MEN AND THEIR WORK
SEVEN

Men like to work. It's in their design.

God is a worker, and we are created in His image. Laziness and non-participation go against everything in the true masculine spirit. Some have erroneously believed that God quit working after creation. He is intensely involved with His creation, working to bring restoration and fullness.

Jesus told some Jews that were persecuting Him for working on the Sabbath, "*My Father is always at His work to this very day, and I, too, am working*" (John 5:17 NIV).

Men can socialize, but the situation has to be right. They need to *do* something.

One of the reasons some men's ministries have failed is because they were structured after the feminine model. I'm sure you've noticed that women can get a lot done over coffee or during "teas." Getting things done for them means hearing, feeling, and sharing. There's a lot of expression taking place.

This expression even leads to spontaneous plans to do good things and service projects. They then actually do them with great precision and effectiveness. It's not uncommon to hear during the Sunday morning announcements that the women have a meeting to share with each other their hearts' desires. And they show up . . . usually in droves.

So the men try to do the same thing and have a Saturday breakfast fellowship. The first few events may draw some men because they want to be involved with other Christian men, but before long many will drop out. They need to have something to *do*.

Men, young and old, are doers! Hearing, sharing, feeling, and expressing won't cut it.

They relate and express themselves through activities like fixing a widow's house, changing the oil in the car of an elderly person, playing golf, basketball, and football, going fishing or hunting, or even strategizing to influence the town.

But men won't engage long if the activity is "just to share." Someone has accurately observed that women relate face to face while men relate shoulder to shoulder.

Some are recognizing the early rumblings of a massive awakening among Christian men. Books are being written about a movement, and they're actually being read. So what does an awakened man look like?

An awakened man understands and celebrates God's design for men. He is comfortable in his own skin. He likes being the man God made him.

For too long, too many men have been bound by expectations to be tame and nice. An awakened man realizes that God has given him permission to be masculine to the fullest degree.

This doesn't mean that he's crude, crass, arrogant, and insensitive. However it does mean that he is free to express his working, warring, worshipping nature with all that's in him.

When you see this kind of man, it's like he's heard a sound in his soul, a battle cry that calls him to be so much more than he appears to be. This call has awakened and confirmed his deepest hope; he can be spiritual AND masculine. He can be righteous, strong, and heroic.

He can appreciate his wife's expression of spiritual intimacy while embracing his own without feeling inferior. He is excited about exploring the depths of masculine worship and nervous but determined to accept a greater role in spiritual leadership in family, church, and community.

The awakened man is also relieved to discover that he has permission to *be called* without joining the clergy. Previously, he may have felt second-class spiritually. There is still a strong religious segment that believes *ordination* not only sets one apart for a specific task in the church, but it conveys a higher level of holiness.

So the idea has been passed on that those in full time ministry have spiritual privileges that others don't have and are somehow closer to God.

As a pastor, I can recount many times when I visited in a home and watched as magazines were hidden, liquor was stuffed under the couch and cigarettes were put out. I appreciate the show of respect for one who represents the gospel of Christ, but I am confident that much of the fear came from believing that, because I was a "man of the cloth," I had some kind of special spirituality.

The same people who could read the magazines, drink their drinks, and smoke without shame in the presence of God felt uneasy in the presence of the *ordained*.

Because they want to be closer to God, to be as spiritually mature as possible, many men have chosen to enter church-related ministry and move out of the marketplace. I don't know the numbers, but from my experience I'd speculate that it would be shocking to discover how many pastors are frustrated because they're not in the right spot.

They've been called to be missionaries to the marketplace, but in their minds, it just doesn't feel as significant.

I want to affirm all those men who have wondered if they were rejected by God or in some way disqualified as spiritual leaders because they work in the business world. God calls us to represent Him in *all* realms of life. Thank God for your place. Don't believe the lie that you're "second-class spiritually." God wants you to follow the call on your life no matter where your assignment takes you.

Awakened men are conscious of living with a commission. They have discovered that the original mandate God gave to Adam is still in effect. They have been commissioned to subdue and cultivate the earth as stewards. That means, like Adam, they have been given a certain garden.

Their garden will require the full use off their gifts, talents, resources, and privileges. As they tend their own garden under the rule of God's kingdom, they subdue that part of the earth. Whether their assignment is in technology, education, agriculture, economics, or any other arena, they are to do their part in extending the rule of the kingdom of God to that area.

It is not just about being bold enough to witness to someone at work. In the minds of many, this is what marketplace ministry is, but it's so much more. Extending the rule of the kingdom of God means kingdom values and practices transform the culture.

What if someone works where there are no unbelievers or there are no people at all? Can his work be distinctively Christian? Of course! It is the work itself that has the marks of Christ on it. Any work done in Jesus' name for His glory is holy work. The quality of the work should shout to the world the superiority of the way of Jesus.

One who works with excellence, compassion, faithfulness, honesty, and diligence is representing Christ. Affecting those around him with joy, purpose, and a love that goes beyond conditions is another step in subduing and cultivating his "garden." And when the purpose of the business itself begins to clearly display the character of God's kingdom, the awakened man's commission is undoubtedly being fulfilled.

The Christian work ethic is not just witnessing at work and making money to give to mission projects. We work because it is how we express our personal worship during most of the week. If we work with a different attitude during the week than we have on Sunday during public worship, we lead duplicitous lives.

We'll be unfulfilled in both work and worship.

This is why so many feel so "secular" during the week and try to be "spiritual" at church. Actually, they feel hypocritical all seven days. The artificial distinction between secular and spiritual must be abandoned. God has come to live in us, making everything we touch spiritual. Holy work is determined by the one who does it rather than the nature of the task.

Digging a ditch for the glory of God is more valuable to God than feeding the poor for personal recognition.

I have had the privilege on several occasions of participating in commissioning ministers to the market place. The purpose is to highlight the significance of this role and its contribution to the body of Christ at large.

I encourage church leaders to take seriously the call of God upon men and women who will never serve on a church staff or become a church officer. Maybe we should *ordain* them to their work. At the very least, let's acknowledge their call and publicly commission them with our blessings and our commitment to *"equip the saints for the work of ministry"* (Ephesians 4:12).

You might ask, "But what about making disciples? Isn't that the Great Commission for all of us?"

Yes. It is the commission we are all given as disciples of Christ, but it is related to the first commission, to subdue and cultivate the earth. We make disciples of Jesus because they will be the ones who can properly subdue the earth for the glory of God.

People who are separated from fellowship with God are limited in their access to the necessary wisdom to steward His earth. Being properly related to God through faith in Jesus Christ gives one the capacity to manage his particular garden with the right motive and the greatest possible success.

We cannot afford to underestimate making disciples of Jesus.

However, we must remember that a disciple is a disciplined person who is intentionally obedient to Jesus. This usually doesn't happen without the personal involvement of someone who leads, mentors, or coaches a young believer into a mature disciple.

The gospel is not about getting individuals to pray a prayer to sign them up for heaven. Entering into a relationship with Christ is great, but making disciples of Jesus is our commission. God's plan has never changed; He wants to transform all of His children into the image of His Son.

It is our privilege to help them become intentional in their God-given assignment. They are the ones who tend the gardens adjoining ours, and only when we all cooperate do we get the job done.

I realize that not everyone agrees with this view.

There are widely-held beliefs out there that tell us
there is not enough time to disciple the nations as
Jesus commanded. They are sure the world is coming
to a quick end and we should take short cuts. They
view long-term planning for changing the whole
world with the whole gospel as unrealistic.

Instead, they're anxious to get their message to every
tribe because they believe that's the key to bringing
Jesus back to earth in judgment. They don't believe
God's original commission to subdue and cultivate
the earth still applies.

They are convinced the earth will burn up anyway
because evil has permeated everything beyond recovery.
Abandoning the created world, they would have us retreat
as we try to snatch as many as possible from eminent
judgment by getting them a ticket to heaven through
praying a quick "sinner's prayer."

I know I've generalized the perspectives of many pastors
and leaders to make a point, but this issue is too important to
ignore. We are grateful for the mercy of God in snatching us
all from a deserved judgment of wrath, but honestly this is a
convoluted perspective of the commission God has given us.

We are under commission of the Lord of all creation.
All that was messed up in Adam's fall has been restored
in Christ's resurrection. History will reveal the success
of this process being applied to all of creation.

In the end, we don't lose anything. Instead, all of creation
will finally experience God's glorious redemption, which

He planned from the beginning. And we are privileged to work with God in bringing about this redemption, not only in preaching the gospel but also in helping others to find their God-given purpose in His world.

We are also commissioned to be fruitful and productive. In the original mandate, the intent was to produce children who would be trained to subdue and cultivate the earth for God's glory. It also included cultivating the land to yield produce and an abundance of natural resources. We are redeemed to continue producing children by natural means as well as through conversion to faith in Jesus Christ. We are also to continue producing a harvest of resources for the development of God's purposes on earth.

So guess what. Hey, men! God has commissioned you to make lots of money. That's right. You are to take dominion over the powers of "unrighteous mammon." Mammon is selfish greed. God wants generous, Christ-centered men to succeed wildly so they can appropriate His resources as a blessing to the whole world.

There's a lot to be done in the restoration project, and God has chosen to use commerce and currency as tools. As men under commission to work with Him on this project, He has given us skills and opportunity to get the resources.

I know, you thought that making money was somehow sinful, or worse, you thought that your skills and opportunities make you somehow a little better than the poor. You're wrong on both counts. You and I are responsible to use all our gifts for the common purpose of honoring the Son. It is all earmarked for redemption.

Don't misuse it.

In fact I must warn you against *dangerous money*. That's the money for which you have no vision or purpose. Surplus riches will rule you. It will call greed from the pits of hell to hobble and hound you until all your joy is gone and you are truly poor.

"Provision" is resources that have been provided to accomplish a vision. If you don't have a vision that matches your resources, you must seek God until He truly enlarges your vision or matches you with someone who has a vision you can join and support.

As you pray, remember there is a difference between a vision and a fantasy. Visions are God-given and will propel you forward even if you can't find the resources you need. Fantasies usually glorify you and justify your greed and hording your wealth.

I have been grieved to watch so many preachers and leaders with vision get sidetracked endlessly raising money, while men with provision get distracted trying to build a ministry for their resources. Why can't they become partners as both contribute their gifts?

One man who had accumulated a nice sum of money decided he wanted to build a ministers' retreat. He bought a beautiful parcel of land and built an expensive and amazing building on it. He then went to the leaders of his denomination and offered the facilities to them for use with their pastors. They looked it over and told him it was not practical for anything they could do. He also offered it to our ministry, and, sadly, we had to tell him the same thing. I have often wished he had partnered with someone who had a vision for that ministry and the two of them could have combined ministry and facility. I think both would have been blessed.

Awakened men are confident in their submission. They have realized that when one in authority sends us, we go as their representatives in their authority.

It's like in the military. When the captain sends the sergeant to take a specific hill, he is granting the authority and resources available to get the job done. Jesus said that He was sending us with the same authority from the Father that sent Him. And unlike human authority, God's authority means guaranteed success (Matthew 28:18).

When Jesus was about to enter Jerusalem for His final week, He told two of His disciples to go across town and get a donkey that was tied at a certain place. He told them if they were asked why they were taking the donkey they were to simply reply:

"The Master has need of it."

Think about that. It's pretty risky. It's like being told to go across town to the local supermarket and find a Mercedes parked there. When you find it, get in the car and drive it back. And if you're caught, tell anyone who tries to stop you that "the Master" has need of it.

The little old ladies in Sunday school never taught me that. When you think about this story, it's hard to make the case that following Jesus is boring or only for nice, timid guys.

Imagine what that must have been like for the disciples. Their adrenalin is pumping. Their eyes are wide open with dilated pupils. They approach the donkey that's tied in the exact spot Jesus said. Slowly they begin to untie him and walk off.

Then their fears come true.

"Hey, what are you doing?"

"Uh, getting this little donkey."

"Yeah, I can see that. Why?"

"Uhh, the Master needs it?"

"Oh, OK. That's fine. Have a good day."

Can you imagine the joy they had as they led that donkey across town with the sense that they had successfully fulfilled their God-given assignment?

Mark this down: if Jesus tells you to go get a donkey, He will make sure you can get the job done.

So here's the question: Where's your donkey, and will you go untie it?

You haven't been left out by Jesus. He has a role for each of us. There is more adventure and excitement waiting for you than Las Vegas ever imagined. It is our privilege to be called into the mission with God. Our "co-mission" is to join Him in His great rescue operation, the redemption of the world.

We work with Him and for Him. That's what we are made for. That's *real* job security. Once you realize that, you'll be comfortable in your own skin.

FOR FURTHER STUDY

1. Why did you start working? Why do you work where you work now? When was the last time you felt God's presence in your work?

2. How does your job contribute to God's mission and the advance of the kingdom of God? Are you pursuing the "co-mission," joining God in His mission for the world?

3. If money were not an issue, where would you work? Why would that allow you to be more effective in coming alongside God in His mission?

CHAPTER
MEN AND THEIR COMMUNITY
EIGHT

There is something about John Wayne that appeals to me.

I know I shouldn't be a loner like the roles he played in his movies, but there is a part of me that would like to be that daring and courageous. For many men, he represents the ultimate hero.

I still enjoy watching his old movies as he saves the day with strength and guts before he rides away into the sunset alone.

But in real life, I've noticed that the roving cowboy is not very happy and not very productive. The strong, silent drifter may prove useful in a crisis, but in the end, he'll break your heart and his.

We weren't meant to be alone. Left to ourselves, we don't work well. You see the best in a man when he's on a team.

Whether we like it or not, we are relational beings. We've been made in the image of God who's always existed in a community. The Father, Son, and Holy Spirit make up the ultimate team. Yes, it's a mystery that our minds cannot totally fathom, but the Godhead is the pattern for mankind.

God said that Adam alone was not good, so He made Eve.

God chose Abraham to have children that would one day become a whole nation.

When Jesus came to earth, He picked twelve men to be His team.

After His death, resurrection, and ascension, He sent a team of gifts to the church to equip the saints for the work of ministry.

His body now is made up of various gifted people who represent Him on earth.

Through the pages of the New Testament, we watch as Paul and his team travel and establish churches through the known world.

It's obvious that God has designed His work to be done through teams of believers.

He didn't give any person all the gifts, and He didn't leave any person without some gift.

One of the reasons for dissatisfaction in the contemporary church is the absence of true teamwork. Local churches are most often led by a singular pastor. He may have a staff of paid or volunteer support, but the real decision making and vision planning come from his personality.

There are various kinds of church government, often designed to share the leadership responsibilities, but the politically astute leader can manipulate the system to get his agenda done.

Consequently, we have burned-out pastors and unused teams.

I am shocked at the pastors and rectors who suffer under the heavy load of delivering the message of God's Word to congregations on a regular basis. What if they tried developing a team approach to study and presentation? What about the heavy loads of counseling and administration? It seems like God's order would work better than the lone-leader approach.

But it's not just the church leadership that suffers from individualism. It paralyzes productivity in every place where teamwork could be employed. The synergy that comes from people working together, sharing in the challenges as well as the rewards, is worth the hassles of communication and coordination.

It's not just the productivity that makes teamwork necessary, however. There is greater joy and fulfillment when the job is shared.

Growing up on a working farm, I looked forward to the times we all worked together. Harvest required teamwork. The hours were long and the work was hard, but the jokes, stories, and shared responsibilities made it seem easier and more fun. I disliked the times when my father (the boss) told me to take the tools and go build a fence or plow a field alone.

There is just something about the team that answers to the vibrations of the soul. I read somewhere that when the great All-Pro quarterback Joe Montana was asked what he missed most about football, his reply was: "The huddle."

It is only when we commit to community that we discover our own gifts and callings. It's easy to fantasize about being a leader until you are placed with others. I have taken a battery of tests that help clarify strengths and weaknesses as well as proclivities. They have been somewhat helpful in knowing what my role in certain teams should be.

But the most direct and accurate way to discover one's role is to get involved with people in doing the job. *They* will let you know.

Have you ever tried out for a competitive team? You might have gone in thinking you would play one part only to find out the team needed you somewhere else.

You have to choose what's more important—your interest or the success of the team.

I attended a relatively small high school in Alabama. Football was very popular, and most of the boys wanted to be on the team. While in the ninth grade I went out for the varsity team, hoping to learn from the older boys. (I was already on the junior varsity.) To my surprise, I actually made the team.

I was the back-up quarterback to the best athlete on the team. I felt pretty safe that my role would be carrying a clipboard and running plays in practice against the first team offense. Graduation had taken all but three players from the preceding year's starting team, so we were a pretty inexperienced group.

The first game was a disaster. The coach decided to move the starting quarterback to running back to give us a better chance to move the ball. The plan meant that I would become the new starting quarterback, though our old quarterback/new running back would call the plays.

Suddenly and unexpectedly I was thrown into the fire. Let's just say it was a learning experience; there were more losses and bruises that year than victories and glory.

The next year, we had a new coach and a new system. I had grown two inches and gained needed weight. The first day of practice coach had all the prospective quarterbacks throwing to our receivers who were running routes.

After practice, the coach and assistants came to me and told me that we desperately needed someone to catch the ball. We had others who could play quarterback even though they had little experience, but we had no one to throw to.

I was "elected" to be a receiver.

Later, I attended a small college on a football scholarship and reported as a receiver. Just before the first game, the coach called me into his office and told me that we were long on receivers and short on tackles. If I would be willing to learn the tackle position, I could be on the starting team instead of a backup receiver.

It was déjà vu all over again.

Even though receivers catch the ball, score touchdowns, and get noticed while tackles block in anonymity on every play, it didn't take me long to decide.

"I'm a tackle," I said. "I want to be on the team."

Those experiences shaped and molded me and have formed my approach when I become a part of any team. Sometimes I am the leader, and sometimes I'm not. That's not the issue; getting the job done and being a part of the team is.

Leaders on one team may be followers on another. True leaders know how to lead from anywhere on the team.

Earlier I referred to our summer program, LEADERSHIP EXPEDITION. It is designed to develop young men into world-changers through instilling wise decision making skills from a biblical worldview.

The men are challenged to learn in the classroom and then apply the curriculum in team-building exercises in a variety of on-site physical activities. Often the one who is the leader in classroom discussion is not the leader in building a bridge or cutting a trail.

One year we had a confident young man who had been a leader in his Boy Scout training to the degree that he had been recognized as a prestigious Eagle Scout. Believing that he was a born leader, he volunteered to be the leader of the work team assigned to build a cedar rail fence in front of the bunk house.

After the first day, his project was in shambles.

The holes were not in line. The men were restless. The posts were put in upside down. Our staff took him out to evaluate the day's work.

"You as the leader are responsible for what your team does," a staff member told him. "This won't do. None of you should be proud of this project."

He was given an opportunity to personally fix the problem and finally admitted that he knew nothing about building a cedar fence. He finally began to act like a real leader. He told his team that he was not qualified and appointed someone who was. For the rest of the week, he dug holes and put up rails. He was an important part of the team that did a tremendous job on the project.

The final result made the team, the staff, and the young man who was willing to change roles proud.

The body of Christ, the community of faith that we all belong to, has a major project a whole lot more difficult than building a cedar fence. We've been given the task of advancing the kingdom of God so that earth becomes a reflection of heaven. It's an overwhelming task that will require exceptional leadership and amazing teams of believers, but it can and will be done.

We'll do it through serving our communities and making disciples of Jesus who can lead, steward, and cultivate the earth under His command. It will take us all. Our objective is way too big for any one person to accomplish. It is bigger than one church can do. It is bigger than one denomination can do.

Someone has accurately concluded that if your vision can be accomplished by you, it is too small. By definition, a leader thinks about more than just himself. We only need a team when our vision requires more than we have to offer.

Maybe our lack of teamwork actually reflects our lack of vision. When we're not trying to doing something truly great, when we don't have God-inspired, supernatural, daring vision, we don't need anybody else.

Discussion of teamwork always causes men to ask about accountability. It sounds frightening.

"Someone is going to be prying around in my life? I don't want anyone to know *everything* about me. I'm ashamed of lots of stuff in my past and there are some things in my life now that are embarrassing."

I know. None of us wants a policeman watching over us, or a detective searching for clues, leads, and suspects. Besides, most of us know how to get around the accountability questions with half-truths and partial answers.

Many men have started out excited about their accountability group only to find that the goal is merely sin management. You know the drill.

"How have you been doing with your pornography issue, Bill?"

"Well, I slipped some this week and I feel terrible."

"OK, let's pray for Bill. Anyone else here having that problem?"

That's better than nothing, but if that's the extent of your accountability, it gets old and it doesn't work. There is hope for transformation in the message of the cross. We must help each other to embrace the cross, the power of the resurrection, and the new life in Jesus led by the Spirit.

Bill's goal is not to just be honest about issues as he confesses his habitual sin, but to overcome them and proactively become the man that God designed him to be: a strong and loving husband, a wise and compassionate father, and a productive and inspiring team member.

Accountability is not something others can enforce on us. We have to want it. Accountability is a trust that we give to others because of our relationship and our common goals.

I don't respond too well to those who have set themselves up as judges of my performance. But when I want to improve or change I must give others the right to help me with perspectives, choices, and priorities.

When I'm paying a golf coach to help me with my swing, he has been given the right to criticize and instruct. I have a goal in mind that's worth being told that I must change. On the other hand, I don't really enjoy the golf partner who is constantly commenting on my game while we're playing a round.

It is an enormous privilege to be a member of the body of Christ. None of us should ever forget that. The opportunity to participate in communicating the Gospel of Jesus to the world is an incredible honor.

Failure to submit to the whole body is failure to submit
to the head (Christ), and that is serious. Excuses are useless.
We must quit whining about how no one recognizes our
gifts. We cannot afford to slink back into the shadows,
excusing our lack of participation because we haven't
been given a chance. We can't ignore the fact that Jesus
Himself put us on His team.

Yes, Christians have hurt you. Yes, leadership has not
been perfect. Yes, it's difficult. But it's still His team. If
we're doing it alone, we are rejecting the orders of our
team captain. So it's difficult. Big deal! We need something
big to do.

Find your spot on the team.

Play your part.

Contribute—not where you want to be, but where
you're needed.

Encourage others who get more recognition than you.

Search for ways to serve the team.

Work at communication and coordination.

It will be worth it a thousand times over. After all, you
are created in the image of the God of community. You are
a team member by creation and redemption.

As you learn to enjoy being a great team member, you'll get

comfortable in your own skin.

1. Specifically describe the best team you've ever been a part of. What made it so great? Now describe your worst team experience. Why was it so difficult?

2. What is the most challenging aspect of working as a team? What part of being on a team is most fulfilling to you?

3. What teams are you a part of right now? What role are you playing? What skills do you need to be effective in that role? What can you do specifically to be a better team member?

CHAPTER
MEN AND THEIR MONEY
NINE

Early in my ministry career, an old deacon pulled a colleague and me aside and gave us a stern word of advice, "There are three subjects you should avoid if you want to be successful as preachers: money, sex, and politics."

I wondered then and now why we should avoid addressing these issues that affect life so dramatically. Should we give in to the tendency to avoid controversy if it causes us to neglect truth that could liberate people?

I'll leave sex and politics for now, but we must address the money subject.

Jesus talked a lot about money. Through parables, practical situations, and interpreting the Law, He taught us how we should use it, how it attempts to use us, and what it means to be a good steward.

So the question we have to ask is, "How does a Christian man handle his money?"

For a lot of people, it's difficult wading through Old Testament customs, laws, and practices trying to understand how they apply to us today.

To make sense of things, some people try to apply the Law literally, which can be really confusing. It's impractical to try to follow all of these regulations—if not impossible—since many of the rules and regulations addressed the theocratic government of Israel and were highly specific to Israel's agricultural economy.

Most of us don't get paid in animals and crops.

At the same time, some people want to discard the Law altogether and just throw it out. But that's a huge mistake too because the Old Testament Law is filled with rich principles of godly wisdom. When we understand and apply these timeless and transcendent truths to our lives, we'll be greatly blessed.

Take the sowing principle. It will be in effect as long as the earth remains (Genesis 8:22).

It teaches us that you harvest *what* you plant.

Then you harvest *more than* you plant. That is one of the primary reasons you should constantly be planting seeds.

Finally, you harvest *later than* you plant.

Good farmers decide what they want to reap and then plant that seed. They wait in hope for the harvest that will provide them with food for their own needs and new seed for planting again.

> The point is this: whoever sows sparingly will also reap sparingly, and whoever sows bountifully will also reap bountifully. Each one must give as he has made up his mind, not reluctantly or under compulsion, for God loves a cheerful giver (2 Corinthians 9:6-7).

Here's another principle to consider: the "first fruits" principle.

It keeps the focus on God, as the ultimate source and center of all economics. By setting aside the first part of the harvest for special honor to God, we must trust Him to make the remainder sufficient. Giving out of surplus does not have the same blessing as giving the first fruits.

The percentage is not so much the priority. Some would have to give a large percentage of the harvest in order to trust God and live by faith. They could even use the tithe ("tithe" means *a tenth* or 10 percent) to substitute for giving in such a way that requires real trust in God.

What is distinct about Christian stewardship? What makes this such a huge issue, a critical battleground between truth and deception? It's more than just following these wise principles. Even non-believers can implement them.

What did Jesus reveal about stewardship that puts it into the supernatural category?

He gives us His own extravagantly generous nature. We have the privilege of living with a sense of unlimited resources. We have been liberated from fears of want and insignificance. Since He demonstrated *a life of giving*, we have a new standard to aspire to.

While the world around us struggles with greed and fear, we can demonstrate the superiority of the kingdom of God on earth through giving as a lifestyle.

This defining characteristic of genuine Christ-like stewardship is literally life-changing.

The New Testament view of giving and stewardship
can be easily summarized: When we walk in genuine
relationship with God, we become like Him . . . and
God is a generous giver!

When we are born of the Spirit, we become partakers of
divine nature (2 Peter 1:1-4). Now we have the "DNA"
of God Himself in us. We, like Him, are givers! We love
to give. We live to give . . . down deep that is. Our "inner
man"is the giver.

We all have a preprogrammed "outer man" since we
lived for awhile under fear (Hebrews 2:14-15). Many of
the popular methods of stewardship are fear motivated, and
fear is what makes us susceptible to false teaching regarding
the curses relating to Old Testament tithes. Fear inevitably
leads to greed. Economic survival will bring out the worst
in fearful people. Greedy people are never happy regardless
of what they possess.

In his letters to the Corinthians, Paul appealed to the new
nature of the Christians in regards to their behavior. They
were to choose actions consistent with their new nature
in Christ.

To fall back into fear of curses as their primary motivation
was to regress. They had the privilege now of displaying to
the whole world the distinct nature of their God. He is the
creator of the universe and has all resources at His disposal,
and He freely gives His resources to those He trusts.

Since we are His heirs, we have been given the privilege of
managing His estate. We operate from a position of wealth

and do not need to fear poverty. Jesus and the gospel of His kingdom are our standards, not the Law.

All the Law and the prophets point to a day when the laws of God would be written on the hearts of His people. When Jesus brought the New Covenant, that day arrived.

> But as it is, Christ has obtained a ministry that is as much more excellent than the old as the covenant he mediates is better, since it is enacted on better promises. In speaking of a new covenant, he makes the first one obsolete. And what is becoming obsolete and growing old is ready to vanish away (Hebrews 8:6, 13).

Our concern is to keep the conditions of the New Covenant. We violate it when we revert back to the law, which was only a placeholder for the day when all people can follow God led by the Spirit. We violate the New Covenant when we try to manipulate the rules in order to be "getters" and "takers" and not "givers." The purpose of giving is not to push the right religious buttons to get more. This isn't the stock market— we don't buy low and sell high.

We live out the New Covenant when we are *joyful, intentional, strategic* givers. Living in the Spirit doesn't mean we don't employ our minds. Led by the Spirit we can thoughtfully manage our resources based on the truth we are given in Christ.

JOYFUL GIVERS

Jesus pointed out the connection between our heart and our

treasure. Therefore, when we give we demonstrate what's most important to us. We are most godly when we give. We are most authentic when we give. There is an internal witness to our act of giving that sends joyful signals throughout our whole being. Giving kicks greed in the teeth and liberates our soul to live beyond the confines of earthly security and significance.

INTENTIONAL GIVERS

A lot of us think, "You know, I really should give someday. I need to do that." When that's our attitude, it won't happen. We must make a committed choice with a definitive plan to follow through.

We could all testify that we can manage to spend whatever we have. We thought we would be content with our financial status when we reached a specific goal, but when we get there we want more. That's how greed works.

But what if we set our giving goal first? Then all of our earning, spending, and saving would be in context with our true purpose in life. The person who is not intentional in becoming a "lifestyle giver" will end up regretting a primarily selfish life.

STRATEGIC GIVERS

It's time to make a plan. For those who just "give when they feel led to give," I can promise that their giving will end up being surprisingly inconsistent and infrequent. Left to ourselves, our human nature has a much greater tendency to "be led" to buy or keep than to give. Of course even the most disciplined and strategic among us have the privilege of being nudged by the Spirit beyond our plans.

Far too many Christians are not yet joyful, intentional, strategic givers.

So what steals the joy of giving from Christians?

A minister friend of mine tells about a man who asked to be coached in living a successful life. When they approached the area of stewardship or resource management, the man revealed that he gave 20% of his income to a local church.

"Why don't you get your life-coaching from your church?" my friend asked.

"Too big," the man replied. "I don't know anyone there who has the time or the inclination."

"So why do you feel compelled to continue to give your money there?" my friend inquired.

The man quickly responded. "Well, I don't want to fall under the curse of not tithing, and I need to keep planting so my finances will be blessed."

You may have heard this idea too. It's not uncommon for local church pastors to teach people to tithe to the church to receive blessings and to avoid the threat of a divine curse. But is this what the Bible teaches?

Typically, the primary text used to support this approach to tithing comes from the Old Testament minor prophet

Malachi. The assumption is to view the local church as the "storehouse" of the Old Testament. In Malachi, the prophet exhorts Israel to bring the tithe(s) to the storehouse.

> Will a man rob God? Yet you are robbing me. But you say, "How have we robbed you?" In your tithes and contributions. You are cursed with a curse, for you are robbing me, the whole nation of you. Bring the full tithes into the storehouse, that there may be food in my house. And thereby put me to the test, says the Lord of hosts, if I will not open the windows of heaven for you and pour down for you a blessing until there is no more need. I will rebuke the devourer for you, so that it will not destroy the fruits of your soil, and your vine in the field shall not fail to bear, says the Lord of hosts. Then all nations will call you blessed, for you will be a land of delight, says the Lord of hosts (Malachi 3:8-12).

It seems simple enough, but we aren't living in the Old Testament era and are not under the blessings and curses of the old covenant.

Malachi was writing to Israel who was guilty of violating their covenant with God. That covenant included a specified system of tithes to take care of the temple, the Levites, and the poor. There were other stipulations in the covenant that Malachi also addressed in his prophecy, such as marriage and divorce and the treatment of Levites.

Malachi was doing what Old Testament prophets do—calling the people to return and obey God during their context in history. He was reminding them of God's covenant with Israel at that time. It included blessings for compliance and curses for disobedience. Violating *any* part of God's covenant brought the curses, not just forsaking the tithe.

I hope you realize that Jesus fulfilled all of God's Law and established a new covenant for us. This is one of the over-arching themes of Scripture. Because of the finished work of Jesus and His new and far greater covenant, we live in a new era.

The *storehouse* of Malachi does not exist in the New Testament economy. Trying to make a local church the equivalent of the Old Testament storehouse reveals a misunderstanding of the present kingdom of God and the nature of the church.

For instance, the Old Testament tithes included taking care of all the Levites who ministered around the temple. Does that transfer over to the New Testament order?

Local churches (and many denominations) are generally built around the pastoral gift, with very little if any emphasis on apostle, prophet, evangelist, and teacher (Ephesians 4:7). Many of the programs of a typical local church are intended to nurture and appease congregants instead of equipping and releasing people to do the work of expanding the kingdom of God on earth.

Therefore, people who desire to engage in kingdom work beyond serving on staff or volunteering for "in house" church work usually find opportunities in extra-local ministries led by apostles, prophets, evangelists, and teachers. These extra-local ministries are not funded by the local church budgets and are often seen by local church leaders to be a competitive drain on the congregation's giving.

If the Old Testament model is being brought over to the New Testament era, then "the Levites" (those receiving the tithe) should include all the ministers involved in equipping the people of God.

The New Testament does not place a high priority on the tithe in the resource management of believers.

Jesus did speak briefly of the tithe. He told the Pharisees (who were still under the old covenant Law) that they should focus on the major things of life, like mercy and justice but not to neglect the tithe (Matthew 23:23). He also mentioned the man who trusted his own righteousness and counted on his tithe as evidence that he deserved God's favor (Luke 18:9-14).

When the apostle Paul spoke of supporting the gospel ministry he appealed to the new nature believers have received in Christ. They are now *givers* and should choose a behavior consistent with their nature (2 Corinthians 9:6-15). The only time he referred back to the Law was to point out that even the oxen were not muzzled as they worked, and that should be instructive about making sure those who are working for the gospel are not muzzled (1 Corinthians 9:8-10).

Paul also mentions the example of the old era when those who were employed to work at the temple were able to share in the sacrificial offerings, and how those who now work sharing the gospel should be taken care of (1 Corinthians

9:13-14). It's interesting that even in this passage he does not mention the tithe.

So why would a church leader teach people to tithe to avoid the curse and insist that the tithe is to be given to the local church? I don't presume to be able to speak with certainty for all pastors, but I can speculate from my own experience.

This perspective was probably taught to them. The view has been around for a long time and has become tradition in many places. Maybe they have not taken the time to carefully study what the Bible says about this issue apart from their particular culture, practice or faith tradition.

It's also possible that they have studied the subject but their method of interpretation does not embrace a progressive view of the nature of revelation in Scripture. They may still be treating the Old Testament as the final instructive authority in ethical behavior. Failure to see the New Testament as fulfilling and explaining the Old will lead to confusing conclusions.

It is easy to use the Old Testament shadows and types as complete and still binding if each law is not taken through the supreme interpreter: Jesus.

Finally, it must be considered that some local church leaders are under pressure to meet budget demands, and this pressure can easily push one toward sloppy biblical interpretation and preserving the traditional perspective.

This kind of teaching does not empower people to be effective stewards of their resources. It makes it difficult to create a healthy environment. Wrong ideas and misguided perspectives often follow: the fear of being cursed, being limited to give exclusively to local church programs, viewing 10% as the standard rather than a starting point for lifestyle giving, or overemphasizing the principle of sowing as a way to get more money.

All of these fall short of the goal—being joyful stewards of the blessings we have been entrusted with from God.

So what is the truth regarding our management of money? Primarily, it is that stewardship is not optional for those who follow Christ. In fact, our destiny is tied to stewardship— the faithful management of what we have been given. The original mandate was to steward and cultivate the earth. It is not ours to abuse for our own selfish ends. It is ours to manage for our master.

A large part of the final accountability all of us will surely face will focus on what we did with what we were given. (2 Corinthians 5:6-10, Matthew 25:14-30). Those who claim to submit to Jesus' Lordship and do not address stewardship have either been fooled or are fooling themselves and will be surprised in the final accounting.

But rest assured that God cannot be fooled, and He leads those who truly know Him out of deception and into liberating truth.

At this point you may ask, "How much should I give?" I encourage you to stretch your faith. Sacrifice some. Extend yourself to give. Make it a priority. Don't settle for writing your 10% tithe bill.

You're not paying for protection from the heavenly hit man. You are privileged to express the nature of the God who lives in you, and you can invest in the only guaranteed work in history. God won't be in debt to anyone, and He promises to give back to those who give so that they can give again.

It should follow that as we walk with God and grow in our understanding of Him, we'll give more and more of what we've been given. Don't worry about where you started; ask yourself if you're giving is growing. Growing in God will mean growing in giving.

You probably also want to ask, "Where should I give?" The general answer is, wherever there is real need.

I realize that this may not help. There are so many needs out there that it can be difficult to discern where your giving can best honor God. So let's look at some guidelines for giving.

Your local church is a good starting point. God is committed to the local church, the representation of His body in the earth. Unfortunately, I'm afraid that not all local churches are worthy of support. However, most are. The presence of the church in a community is a prophetic word to society.

If you aren't sure your church is properly representing God's kingdom, get involved enough to know. I beg you, though: Don't give just to dodge curses. Don't give irresponsibly. Don't give without personal involvement. Second, God has used certain people and ministries to get you where you are. They should have a priority in your giving too. *"One who is taught the word must share all good things with the one who teaches"* (Galatians 6:6).

God has sovereignly arranged for certain lives to interact and to partner for His glory and the advance of His kingdom. You will experience great joy and satisfaction as you give with gratitude for God's mercy shown through the ministries that have blessed you.

Give to ministries that share your values, mission, and vision. You may have a heart for certain people-groups, a particular cause or mission, or a certain message that you are passionate about declaring. Don't overlook those less-publicized expressions of the gospel, because the size of the organization doesn't determine its worth. And remember, your finances are just one of the resources that you are responsible to manage; your time, your prayers, your energy, and your passion can all be invested as well.

But above all in your giving and your living, PROCLAIM THE GOSPEL. When you can't do it yourself, support those who can.

There are many important causes vying for our attention. The family is important. Public policy is important. Caring for the widow and the orphan is important. But the gospel is the only power of God unto salvation. If the gospel does not precede or accompany any ministry, it will not succeed. History shows that when the gospel is effective, all aspects of society are blessed.

The message of God's kingdom coming in Jesus the Christ is priority. The only hope of change and transformation is the gospel. At times, it has been diluted by those seeking wide popularity and public fame. It has been denied by those afraid of its demands and challenging truth. It has been dissected by those who prefer to discuss it rather than live it. But it must be the center of our focus, and therefore, at the core of our giving. We must never forget that just communicating religious content is not preaching the gospel.

Discipleship is the goal.

We are told by Jesus to preach the gospel with a view to making disciples of Jesus. If we aren't doing that, our ministries are in vain.

Discipleship doesn't take place just from the pulpit or the podium. It happens when people in relationships, based on their common faith, seriously love one another.

As you mature as a steward and a manager of resources, you should grow in your discipline in areas like spending, saving, investing, and borrowing. There are numerous resources available for guidance in each of these subjects that a genuine disciple and serious learner should pursue.

I have been truly amazed to see that, when the focus of finance changes from being the owner to being the manager, all the aspects of economics change.

Christian men are tired of being manipulated regarding their money. They want their giving to be an expression of worship. They don't want to be disrespected and dishonored by being used as "cash cows" and then expected to tolerate inefficient and ineffective programs. They want to be partners with all those who live to give to see the kingdom of God expressed both in this generation and those to come. They know that, down deep, a man comfortable in his skin is a *giver*.

FOR FURTHER STUDY

1. What does Scripture mean when it says the love of money is "the root of all sorts of evil"? (1 Timothy 6:10)

2. What does Jesus mean when He describes "mammon"? (Matthew 6:24, Luke 16:9-13 NKJV)

3. How important is Christian stewardship in relation to the gospel? What kind of steward have you been? What kind do you want to be?

4. Do a thorough study of 2 Corinthians 8-9 and develop a plan for your personal stewardship.

CHAPTER
MEN AND TRANSFORMATION
TEN

There are four questions that demand an answer before you read this chapter.

Do you need to change?

If so, what do you need to change?

Do you want to change?

How bad do you want it?

The gospel of Jesus Christ offers hope for change—a change as radical as resurrection from the dead.

It is not easy, but it is possible. It cost Jesus dearly, so it isn't cheap or trivial. It goes far beyond new resolutions and bullet points, three-step sermons and fancy formulas. Men can change. Not just some habits, but at the core of their being, they can become what God intended when they were created and redeemed.

Many of the issues that divide the church today can be reduced to the question of whether or not people can really change. Sanctification, the process of genuine life transformation of the growing believer, is not always the highest priority of every church. A consumer oriented church will tend to leave people unchanged while using them to build successful organizations.

Maybe one of the saddest and most dangerous beings on earth is a person who is Christian in name but not in heart. Unchanged religious hypocrites tarnish the true hope that is central to the gospel of Jesus' death and resurrection.

Our hope for new life and redemption hinges on these kinds of questions: Can abused people be restored to health? Can addicted people be freed to live productively? Can sexually confused people find clarity in their God-ordained identity?

If not, then the best we can do is comfort permanently sick people in their hopeless condition and offer them the deferred hope of a better life in heaven someday.

You don't hear too much talk these days about mankind's sinful nature. People don't have character flaws and sinfulness. They have "issues."

I was visiting with a young woman sitting beside me on a flight back to Dallas. She began telling me about her financial dilemma. She had a good job but could not make ends meet—she never had enough money at the end of the month. Finally, she admitted that she had a "shoe issue." She had over one hundred pairs of shoes in her closet and was compelled to buy more each time she went shopping.

That's certainly an issue, but without change it will grow to become something more dangerous.

However, at some level, I understand. All of us have issues. It doesn't require personal responsibility to admit the existence of an issue. Some people even take pride in their issues.

But sooner or later we handle our issues or they handle us. Issues need to be addressed, and someone has to take responsibility if we're going to find a solution.

Working through our issues is not about assigning blame. How the issue got to be an issue is not nearly as important as getting help. Neglecting the salvation provided in Christ has the same effect as rejecting it. The gift must be received.

Let's visit some of the common ways we approach our "issues." First, we can hide them. We convince ourselves that they don't exist, or we can compensate for them through intricate explanations and excuses. This may work well for awhile, but posing is tiring and eventually we can't handle the shame.

The truth is that others rarely believe what we pretend to be. In trying to deceive others, we end up deceiving ourselves. People see through the phony stuff we try to sell.

Second, we change the standards. If we can't measure up to what is considered healthy, we lower the standards. Diseases that can't be cured are no longer considered diseases. Defeat is incorporated into the norm of life. Debilitating addictions that were once considered embarrassing are accepted as ordinary and common.

It may momentarily take away the social pressure, but it deteriorates our quality of life. Victimized by our flaws, we are left to make the best of a bad situation. Childhood scars define us for a lifetime. Injustices shape our personalities. The events of our past and the actions of others mold us, leaving no real hope of becoming what God originally designed for mankind.

We do have a third option—we can trust God to change us. But this will require us to identify what we want to change, address it, and refuse to give in until change comes. That means we own our wrong doing, repent, and choose to walk away from destructive behavior and wrong thinking.

I realize this is not the popular answer because it's rarely a quick fix. It will require a radical commitment and some long obedience in the same direction.

But it can be done.

There are enough testimonies from reliable witnesses out there to validate this hope. You can probably think of several who tried and didn't make it, but it only takes one life that God changed to destroy the myth that it's impossible.

God's method of change is not about willpower or trying harder. It requires desperation and brokenness. You'll never change what you are willing to tolerate.

The key is to focus on the person God is changing you into and not the version of you that you want to change. You won't say "no" to an idol who offers some satisfaction to your desires, until you have said "yes" to the true God who satisfies your deepest desires.

Satan's temptation is to offer illegitimate fulfillment to our legitimate desires.

We all know it's not wrong to eat, sleep, rest, have sex with a wife or husband, work, or play. But when these are meeting needs that go beyond their design, we have moved into disorder and we become susceptible to addiction. When

the substitute doesn't completely satisfy, more and more
is required.

For instance, the sex drive is only satisfied when incorporated into a committed relationship with a marriage partner
of the opposite sex. If this drive is pursued outside of God's
intended environment, it will demand more and more until it
drives our life. The same goes with work, food, success, and
the remainder of our God-given drives.

Most of us can testify that resolve alone doesn't work.
Failing again to keep our commitments only adds to the
shame that already weighs us down. We learn from the
apostle Paul's teaching that one of the primary purposes
of the Law was to expose our inability to live righteously
on our own. It was a kind of mentor to lead us to salvation
in Christ (Romans 6 and 7).

> We know that our old self was crucified with him
> in order that the body of sin might be brought to
> nothing, so that we would no longer be enslaved to
> sin . . . So you also must consider yourselves dead
> to sin and alive to God in Christ Jesus. Let not sin
> therefore reign in your mortal bodies, to make you
> obey their passions. Do not present your members
> to sin as instruments for unrighteousness, but
> present yourselves to God as those who have been
> brought from death to life, and your members to
> God as instruments for righteousness. For sin will
> have no dominion over you, since you are not under
> law but under grace (Romans 6:6, 11-14).

Notice first, that if we're in Christ we've been crucified; we're dead. Who wants to die? Only those who've realized and accepted they cannot do it on their own.

It should be noted that Jesus didn't come to help us be better at what we are already doing. He is not about *aiding* us. God has concluded that we are so infected by sin that death is the only cure. We will never get well by anything else.

That's really bad news if death is the end. But the good news of the gospel is that Jesus died in our place. He not only paid the *penalty* of our sins, He also destroyed the *power* of sin. Therefore, when we die to sin, it no longer has any power over us. When we die, we can finally live— but only if we're living by faith in Christ.

> It is no longer I who live, but Christ who lives in me. And the life I now live in the flesh I live by faith in the Son of God, who loved me and gave himself for me (Galatians 2:20).

When we are sick enough of our issues and the ineffectiveness of our efforts to manage our lives, we have an opportunity to really live. However, it takes a broken, honest man to die to ourselves and live for Christ.

As a first-year seminary student I became the pastor of a small church. One day I received a call from a man from church, named Bill. He calmly told me that he was about to take his life.

He wanted to know if I would still perform his funeral if he committed suicide.

How do you answer a question like that? Despite how I was feeling on the inside, I realized I needed to stay calm. I told him that performing funerals was part of my job, so if he died, I would fulfill my duty.

I was hoping and praying it wouldn't come to that. I asked him to come by and talk with me—I didn't want the next time I saw him to be in a casket. He reluctantly agreed on the condition that we would talk in his car and not in my office.

Bill was a large, healthy-looking man. His body was marked with many tattoos, and in the 70s they weren't as stylish or trendy as they are today. His glasses were very thick. His hair was well-cut and styled, and you could smell the Vitalis (hair tonic).

He told me his story. It was a surreal experience; like listening to a suicide note from a man who hadn't yet carried it out.

He dropped out of school early because of a learning disability. Without a basic education, he had no skills that were marketable. It followed that he had subsequently had several run-ins with the law.

In addition to these challenges, he had a degenerative eye disease that left him with just 20% of vision. He knew he'd be blind in the immediate future. His condition was so serious that the doctors warned him his retina could detach with only the slightest pressure, which meant he could not do manual labor.

He had several children, a lovely wife, and no way to provide for them.

Bill was a broken man.

He explained that because he couldn't take care of his family and things were only getting worse, the best thing he could do would be to take his own life. That way his wife, who was still young, would be free to marry a man who could take care of her and the children who were also showing symptoms of the eye disease.

As he finished telling me his heart-wrenching story, hoping he was bluffing and wondering how close he was to actually going through with it, I inquired to see how ready he really was.

"How are you proposing to do this?" I asked.

He reached into the glove compartment and retrieved a 38 caliber revolver. From the look in his eye I knew he wasn't playing games.

"Oh, that will be messy" I said. "What if your children see pictures of that?"

"Well, what do you suggest?" he asked desperately.

By this point I was flying totally by the seat of my pants. Actually, I had long since left areas of ministry that I had ever been trained to handle. They don't exactly cover scenarios like this in your first few seminary courses. But I had to do something.

"Well, since you can't see a way out and you're ready to die, why don't you trust the death God has already provided for you?" I suggested.

I gave it everything I had. "God has a way for you to give up the control of your life, and He said that when we do this, He takes the responsibility for your future. What have you got to lose? If God kills you . . . well, you're about to kill yourself anyway in an awful mess. But God can do what you can't—He can give you new life. And when He does, He's responsible to provide all the resources you need."

"I didn't know about that" he said. "How do I do it?"

"Let's pray, and you tell God that you accept Jesus' death as yours . . . that your relinquish control of your life to Him and will accept whatever verdict He has, life or death, for your future."

Bill bowed his head and prayed that simple prayer. He then looked up with a terrifying and appropriate question.

"What do I do now? I have never been dead before."

The Holy Spirit was literally transforming history in the front seat of Bill's car, but I didn't really know how to answer the question. So I reached in my pocket and handed him three cards with Scripture verses on them that I had been memorizing.

He looked at me like I was crazy. "I can't memorize anything! That is one reason I dropped out of school."

"Yes you can," I insisted. "Your old life has died, remember? Have these memorized by Sunday. Come by my office before church."

He took the cards, came on Sunday and stumbled through them. I gave him more. He got those done too. In fact over the next 24 months he memorized several hundred verses of scripture.

Since he was "dead" and he didn't have a job, he had lots of time to spend with me. He went to hospitals, jails, youth camps, and pastoral visiting. Just like we prayed, God began to provide the resources he needed.

He took my job at the jails after he noticed that I wasn't really too comfortable there. After all, he had been in jail before and immediately identified with the inmates.

For the next 20 years Bill continued that prison ministry. During that time he completed his GED, became the pastor of a church in the area with great success. He still ministers today, his children are grown, and his family is whole.

Bill found there is life after death.

Like Bill, apart from God we come up with crazy and dangerous solutions. We tend to believe we can succeed if we try a little harder, compensate a little more, and get a little help.

Here's the key: Once we finally consider ourselves dead in Christ, that's not the end. It's "dying," but it's not giving up. You don't immediately go to live with Jesus in heaven.

We must then present the members of our body as instruments of righteousness. It's not just stopping bad behavior . . . it's about living righteously. It's not about what you've stopped doing but what you've started to do.

We are all familiar with the way addictions grow. We are tempted by some illegitimate answer to our desires, and the first time there is a battle with our conscience. The next time the battle is less intense and so on until there is no battle at all. We have become slaves of that offer.

I have never heard anyone say they were addicted to pornography the first time they were exposed. Many testify of the mixture of excitement and/or shame of the first experience, but it took yielding several times before the obsession was complete.

In the same way we can employ the new life in us now that we have trusted in Christ's death and resurrection. We choose to yield our members (mind, eyes, hands, body, etc.) to acts of righteousness. It may take a while to develop an addiction to righteousness, but over time it becomes just as natural as our unrighteous issues.

As we choose to act in faith, He works in us to perform what we could never do alone. Before long, we do it without even thinking about it.

Our goal in the process of change is to build what Paul calls the "inner being":

> For this reason I bow my knees before the Father, from whom every family in heaven and on earth is

named, that according to the riches of his glory he may grant you to be strengthened with power through his Spirit in your inner being (Ephesians 3:14-16).

We have some leftover programming in us. Paul calls it flesh, not because he believed the material world was sinful, but because it reflects the nature of our focus. The flesh gratifies itself at the expense of others. Life in the Spirit always glorifies God and blesses everyone.

But I say, walk by the Spirit, and you will not gratify the desires of the flesh. For the desires of the flesh are against the Spirit, and the desires of the Spirit are against the flesh, for these are opposed to each other, to keep you from doing the things you want to do. But if you are led by the Spirit, you are not under the law (Galatians 5:16-18).

Notice that the flesh responds to the law. That is why self-effort to improve and live up to higher standards will only excite the flesh. The end result will be disappointment. We can only change by the power of the One who raised Jesus from the grave.

God has His ordained means of grace. In other words, there's a clear, biblical process that we can trust to change us.

Here's a brief overview: (1) Complete trust in Jesus as the Christ sent to deliver us from our sins; (2) Absolute reliance on the cross of Jesus to pay the penalty of our sin and defeat the powers of sin in us today; (3) Committed involvement in His multi-gifted community called the Church; (4) Strategic plan to build the inner being while decreasing the influence of the flesh.

Trying to change without these may have some measure of temporal change. But the distinctively biblical approach to transformation always includes all four of these components.

Let me ask you some questions, so that you will have the confidence to know that God will transform you:

Have you settled the issue of Jesus Christ alone being your Savior and Lord?

Have you appropriated his death and resurrection as your own?

Are you connected with other believers in an accountable relationship? Who has a right to speak into your life? What is his name? Cell number?

What disciplines are you putting into your life right now? Do you have a scheduled time for prayer and meditation? Does your calendar reflect a regular commitment to the spiritual disciplines like worship, work, recreation, solitude, silence, and self-denial?

Remember, a neglected salvation has the same effect as a rejected salvation. *"How shall we escape if we neglect such a great salvation? It was declared at first by the Lord, and it was attested to us by those who heard"* (Hebrews 2:3).

CHANGE IS A JOURNEY

We will never get there if we don't start. The cross and empty tomb of Jesus are the sources of our hope. There is nothing wrong with us that death and brand-new life cannot fix. You can change. Your family can change. Your neighbor can change. The world can change.

And when men are in the process of being transformed into the image of God's Son, they'll be comfortable in their skin.

FOR FURTHER STUDY

1. Why do you think people despise hypocrites? If we're honest, aren't we all hypocritical at some level? Why?

2. Do you believe there are issues, addictions, or perversions that cannot be corrected? Why?

3. What is the most difficult area of change you personally have encountered? What made this so hard?

4. What area of your life needs to be transformed right now? What area would you like to change in the next year?

"MIS-NAMING"

CHAPTER
MEN AND MANAGEMENT
ELEVEN

If we take the Bible at its word, you can't avoid the idea that God gave man responsibility over the earth to manage, steward, and cultivate it as an act of worship.

God specifically gave that assignment to Adam, and by extension, all of mankind:

> Then God said, "Let us make man in our image, after our likeness. And let them have dominion over the fish of the sea and over the birds of the heavens and over the livestock and over all the earth and over every creeping thing that creeps on the earth" (Genesis 1:26).

Jesus reiterates this theme over and over in His parables — God gives man resources to manage, He waits, and then He either rewards or punishes their stewardship.

Discussion remains, however, on whether or not Jesus actually expects mankind to accomplish this.

Some people believe that the earth will only be subdued and cultivated after the church is removed from the earth, when Jesus Himself comes with immortal saints and angels to rule over the earth.

Others believe that Jesus has done what is necessary to rule, and He does this through His body. I believe the latter.

Let's be honest; the first scenario is a whole lot easier. We get to relax knowing that we have no responsibility in making any difference in history. If we know things will inevitably get worse, there is nothing meaningful to do regarding the constructive stewardship of things, until the intervention of heaven. So we could singularly focus on making sure we're ready for the judgment.

Think of it this way—an irresponsible renter doesn't care for their house; a diligent owner does . . . I know, we are not owners, but we represent Him.

If I'm just a renter, the deterioration of societal structures like the family, the community, and even the nation aren't my problem. If justice in this world is not possible, then there's nothing we can do about the suffering of children, widows, and orphans. If peace only comes after Jesus returns, then we don't need to worry about violence destroying lives all around the world.

Too many Christians have adopted this view, and it has become a self-fulfilling prophecy.

But as salt of the earth and light of the world, I believe we have the privilege of working with the ruling King to influence the world and be a part of its restoration. A renter looks the other way, but owners role up their sleeves and get to work.

But what does that practically look like? And perhaps more importantly, how can we be a part of this? In order to accomplish the task God gave Adam, he was given authority and the ability to manage God's created earth.

> Then the Lord God said, "It is not good that the man should be alone; I will make him a helper fit for him." So out of the ground the Lord God formed

every beast of the field and every bird of the
heavens and brought them to the man to see what
he would call them. And whatever the man called
every living creature, that was its name. The man
gave names to all livestock and to the birds of the
heavens and to every beast of the field
(Genesis 2:18-20).

Notice that he named the animals and knew their nature
enough that none were picked as his helpmate. He could tell
the true nature of things and was able to distinguish one
from the other.

I think we can safely say that *mankind will not be able
to manage the earth if he can't name the animals*. In other
words, if a man can't tell the difference between a gorilla
and a pig, he's going to have a difficult time making good
leadership decisions.

Wisdom is the ability to identify the nature of things and
then position them for their greatest possible productivity
or fruitfulness.

God is a master artist. He specifically and uniquely created
all life with microscopic detail according to His great design.
He doesn't encourage one species to act like another. He
gives everything He creates a unique nature, a purpose,
and an ideal way of life.

Science has determined there are distinct kingdoms of
reality: the mineral kingdom, the plant kingdom, the animal
kingdom, and the human kingdom. It is interesting that to

change kingdoms, a thing has to die to its identity in the previous kingdom.

A mineral gives up its distinction as a mineral to be a part of the plant when nutrients in soil are absorbed to make plants grow. The plant gives up its nature to become part of an animal when a cow chews and digests grass. And in turn, the animal gives up its nature to become a part of the human kingdom when it becomes a steak on my plate.

In order for us to steward and cultivate the earth, we need to apply the same wisdom Adam used to name the animals when we manage the earth's resources. Left to our devices, human wisdom is limited by what we can observe as we test the events in life. That's why people end up fighting to protect spotted owls and humpback whales while we neglect to manage and care for people.

But there is a higher wisdom that comes from God.

Human observations must be aided and interpreted by divine perspective in order to steward and cultivate the earth as God intended. In order for us to understand the purpose and position of the things in this world, we need the perspective and commentary from the One who created them.

History is a record of events that can be recorded to prove any number of perspectives or agendas. Unless history is interpreted by someone who knows the beginning from the end, the big picture significance and the consequences of moments and events escape us.

Abram was a man who lived in the Middle East several thousand years ago. He left his homeland on a journey. Why is that significant? Many inhabitants of Ur had made trips before. But this one was initiated by God in His purpose to rescue the human race and restore the earth to its original purpose.

It becomes part of the divine story of redemption that is culminated in Jesus the Christ. We understand the significance only when we have God's perspective—we call this perspective, *wisdom*.

Years later, several million descendants of Abraham left Egypt and wandered in the desert. Other tribes had left one part of the world for another. What does this event have to do with you and me?

It was the Exodus, the defining event of the ancient world that the Old Testament refers to over and over. God was working miraculously in the lives of His people as a foreshadow of the great Passover (from sin) and Exodus (from the fall of man and the power of sin and death) for all mankind.

Later, a man dies outside the walls of Jerusalem. Many had done that before, and many would do that later. Why was this significant? Would anyone have known if God had not commented on it?

Wisdom is the divine perspective necessary to do our job on earth.

The age of David and Solomon is known as the Golden Age of Israel. Solomon's name is associated with true wisdom. He exhibited the ability to look beyond what everyone else saw to see the true nature of things and then make the perfect decision.

People came from all over the known world to marvel at his wisdom. We have several books in the Bible that are commonly referred to as the wisdom books: Job, Proverbs, Ecclesiastes, and Song of Solomon. Each one gives a different view of wisdom, but all point to a heavenly wisdom that is possible when God adds His perspective to life on earth.

The hope of Israel included a belief that one day there would be a new kind of wisdom given to God's people. They believed that it would be a part of the Day of the Lord when He judged His enemies and vindicated His people.

After the age of David and Solomon, things went badly for Israel. They began to neglect the wisdom of God and gradually lost the ability to rule over themselves and the land they had been given. When they lost God's perspective, they lost wisdom—the ability to see the true nature of things and make the right decisions.

Finally, they were ruled over by foreign powers and ended up in captivity. It seems they refused to name God as God alone and ended up not being able to name anything correctly. Their destruction can be explained in Paul's depiction of mankind's inevitable disintegration.

> For although they knew God, they did not honor him
> as God or give thanks to him, but they became futile
> in their thinking, and their foolish hearts were
> darkened. Claiming to be wise, they became fools,
> and exchanged the glory of the immortal God for
> images resembling mortal man and birds and
> animals and reptiles (Romans 1:21-23).

Whenever someone refuses to recognize God as God, they
become confused about the nature of everything. All kinds
of crazy thoughts start to sound reasonable as they confuse
what has been created with the Creator.

From the early stages of confusion and depravity, reason
begins to spiral in on itself to the degree that people confuse
the nature of male and female, and even begin to accept
animals as sex partners for humans. The last straw in this
destructive process is the inability to tell the difference
between good and evil.

Though not every human has taken this to the ultimate possible extreme, we are all in that descent toward destruction
when we don't have God's wisdom. All of us are prone to
idolatry. We are dangerous to ourselves and to our society
when we are left without God's wisdom.

Some obvious consequences of our unwise perspective
are the disappointments that result from wrong expectations.
We have misnamed something or someone and become
upset when they could not perform to our standards.

Wives have named their husband "savior" and been
disappointed when he couldn't save. Husbands have named

their wife "mama" and then blamed her for not being mama.
We name our church leaders "perfect" and then condemn
them for being human. We name our churches "utopia" and
then criticize when it proves to be a family of imperfect
people seeking to learn how to embrace God.

Added to our long list of disappointments is our record
of poor productivity. God has designed our projects to
be completed by teams. When we refuse to name the
team members accurately and give positions rather than
assignments according to gifts and talents, we don't get
the jobs done.

Critical and judgmental attitudes and constant widespread
frustration are clear indicators of poor management that
lacks the wisdom of God.

Speaking of frustration, I enjoy playing golf on occasion.
I have one specific memory from several years back. You
should know first that one of the things that drew me to
the game was the dignity and integrity of golf.

Like anything worthwhile, in order to be good you have
to work hard and make an investment of time and resources.
I realized that I was not in a position to make that kind of
commitment so I adjusted my expectations; I chose to be
a man who plays golf instead of trying to be a golfer.

There's a big difference between the two. Most people can't
see their true nature on the golf course.

On this particular day, I played with a man who grew so
frustrated that he bent his club around a tree and started

hyperventilating. I was doing my usual thing of hitting a few good shots and then several not so good shots, but because my expectations were appropriate, I was enjoying myself despite my shortcomings.

I loved being with the foursome—we were telling good stories and having a great time laughing at each other's lack of ability. The frustrated man came over and cornered me.

"I know you're competitive. You like to win." (He had been talking with my wife, I suppose.) "Why are you able to laugh this off? Don't you care that you're not winning?"

I explained to him that when it came to the golf course, I knew who I was. I didn't expect to play like a pro. I knew I was a duffer. To expect anything better would be stupid. If at some point I chose to really work at it, I would have to invest a great deal of my time and resources in order to expect to shoot a competitive score.

Don't hear that being average in everything is OK. But do hear this: Wisdom allows you to see the true reality of things and name them accordingly.

A gorilla is not a pig, and a duffer doesn't break par (unless he cheats really bad).

Jesus was the fulfillment of Israel's long anticipated new wisdom. Jesus the Messiah is the wisdom of God. He demonstrated what God's perspective looks like in human form. For instance, He knew who believed and who didn't.

> But Jesus on his part did not entrust himself to them,
> because he knew all people and needed no one to
> bear witness about man, for he himself knew what
> was in man (John 2:24-25).

Jesus could tell when a storm needed to be rebuked and
when it needed to be enjoyed.

He knew when an affliction required the expulsion of a
demon and when it was a disease that needed to be healed.

He knew that Lazarus was to be raised but others in the
same cemetery were not.

He knew that the man born blind was for the purpose of
showing the glory of God.

He named Simon "Peter" (the rock) even when he blew
like a reed in the wind.

He knew who Judas was and was neither surprised nor
frustrated when he acted out of his nature.

He operated as a man with the wisdom of God. He could
look through and past what everyone else saw to see the
true nature of things.

He never "misnamed the animals."

He lived among a religious people who had badly misnamed
reality. They had refused to name the Messiah and therefore
had misnamed themselves. They were confused as to the

nature of righteousness. They thought being a Jew was the basis of being in God's family.

They couldn't recognize the temple when it was among them. They did not name the times correctly and were destroyed by a Roman army they could have avoided if they had had God's perspective.

Misnaming Jesus cuts one off from the wisdom that comes from God. Paul tells us the secret to the new wisdom:

> Yet among the mature we do impart wisdom, although it is not a wisdom of this age or of the rulers of this age, who are doomed to pass away. But we impart a secret and hidden wisdom of God, which God decreed before the ages for our glory. None of the rulers of this age understood this, for if they had, they would not have crucified the Lord of glory. But, as it is written,
>
>> "What no eye has seen, nor ear heard, nor the heart of man imagined, what God has prepared for those who love him" —
>
> these things God has revealed to us through the Spirit. For the Spirit searches everything, even the depths of God (1 Corinthians 2:6-10).

The wisdom that Adam had tasted, that Solomon had foreshadowed, and that Israel had longed for came in the person of Jesus.

He not only has wisdom, He is wisdom.

It is relational, not just intellectual. Wisdom is not something
we know; it's who we're in relationship with. When we
come to be included in Him, we have access to the perspective that makes the world make sense.

> He is the source of your life in Christ Jesus, whom
> God made our wisdom and our righteousness and
> sanctification and redemption (1 Corinthians 1:30).

When we walk in relationship with Jesus, He'll give us His
perspective. He'll let us see the purpose of history, the nature
of salvation, the identity of God's people, the power of the
gospel, and the reality of God's kingdom.

Anything we view without His perspective is suspect at best.
Any truth that is applied apart from Jesus won't prove to
be wise in the long run. Any advice we receive that ignores
Christ is man's advice. He alone is the one mediator between
God and mankind.

All truth from God comes through Jesus. And it is available
to the "in Christ" people. They simply have to ask.

> If any of you lacks wisdom, let him ask God, who
> gives generously to all without reproach, and it
> will be given him. But let him ask in faith, with
> no doubting, for the one who doubts is like a wave
> of the sea that is driven and tossed by the wind
> (James 1:5-6).

Can we get back to the original assignment of managing the earth? It's the God-given responsibility of all mankind.

We have been rescued by God, and He has made the necessary wisdom available in Christ. We, by His revelation, can discern the true nature of things and people, and we can know how to manage in relation to them. When we fulfill this role that we were created for, we'll be filled with supernatural joy. There's nothing quite like doing what you were designed to do.

We get to walk in the presence of God and work in His wisdom to accomplish what He had in mind when He created mankind. Jesus, being the ultimate human, has done what is necessary for us to be empowered to succeed. When we live in Christ, it gives Him glory and it gives us dignity.

It makes us fully human—men comfortable in their own skin.

FOR FURTHER STUDY

1. Describe Adam before the fall. What did wisdom look like then? What keeps us from God's wisdom now?

2. Name two specific wise insights from Proverbs that have had an impact on your life. What blessing of wisdom described in Proverbs do you need in your life right now?

3. What is the book of Ecclesiastes about? What makes it challenging to study?

4. Why don't we believe that God will give us wisdom? If you need help, look at James 1:5-11. Which part of the passage describes your struggle most accurately?

CHAPTER

MEN AND THEIR CONFIDENCE

TWELVE

I've been training two dogs lately, and in the process I'm learning more about myself than the dogs.

One of the dogs is a strong, dominant Lab whose confidence is high — at least in his own mind. The other is a male English Pointer who lacks confidence and needs to know he can trust his handlers.

The Lab, of course, is more fun to watch even though he's quite the handful. He is never without his own opinion as to how things are to be done, and he believes his opinion is the best. He would be glad to take the whistle and set the agenda for training me. There is never a look of defeat in his eyes.

The English Pointer takes just as much time, however, as I try to "bold him up." He doesn't yet know where to find the source of confidence. It's hard to watch him struggle to find confidence — none of us like to see animals or humans struggle through life intimidated and insecure.

Confidence is attractive. It can also be dangerous.

We all gravitate to the person who has the "look." (Who wants to follow the person who looks like he is lost or confused?) The danger comes from such leaders having confidence in the wrong source combined with our innate need to follow a leader.

History tragically proves that there is always a crowd who will follow confident people even if they are destructive to everyone and everything.

The confidence I am looking for is confidence before God. Scripture tells us that there is a place before God where we can stand without shame and condemnation. It is a place where we trust the acceptance and unconditional love of our generous Father.

Our security and significance come out of our relationship with God, who not only loves us completely but allows us to join Him in spreading the news of His kingdom on earth.

If this is true, and we know that it is, why don't more Christians have confidence?

Mankind was created to be confident before God. It's part of our divine design. Without confidence before God, mankind is incomplete and dissatisfied. Looking at Adam before the fall, we see man comfortable in his position with God. He knows he is the created and not the Creator. He is the working partner on "project earth." He enjoys fellowship with God even in his naked state.

He's not hiding anything.

Then, of course, we have an even better picture of the model man in Jesus. He is the last Adam and reveals what it looks like when a man lives in constant fellowship with the Father. He only does what the Father tells Him to do. He lives with an unwavering confidence as He carries out the Father's plan despite the temptation, distraction, and pressure that surround Him.

This is our hope.

When we are in Christ, we have been granted by grace to have the same relationship with the Father that Jesus has. This relationship is more intimate and better than Adam had before his choice to break fellowship with God.

The tragedy of sin is that it robs us of all confidence before God.

Now, any confidence based on anything other than grace is not only false confidence but an idol standing in the place of our practical worship. All of us have been born into sin, and sin places us into a perpetual state of shame. The tell-tale sign of shame is the insatiable need to fix ourselves.

We want to look better both inside and out. Billions are spent on physical improvements from "botox" to face lifts to tummy tucks, all intended to give new confidence with a new look. Americans also spend billions of dollars each year on psychological therapy in an attempt to fix what is wrong internally.

Sadly, many churches have turned to psychology to find the self-improvements the congregants demand without ever presenting, or at least downplaying, the transforming power of the gospel of Jesus.

Some work on the body and some work on the soul, in the never-ending attempt to undo the damaging effects of shame. If we can't be confident, we must at least look confident.

We have also found plausible substitutes for confidence. For instance, we have discovered that control works for a while when confidence is not available. If we can just get everyone on our page—manipulation, guilt, fear—anything will work to get our agenda on top.

We complicate matters even more when we do all this "in the name of love." Even our love got bent in the fall. Now we can't even do that without a selfish intent. We worship for our benefit. We work for our resources. We play for our pleasure. We love in order to feel good and get our way.

And then we derive a sense of confidence in our ability to manipulate others with our selfish love. We sometimes even convince them we're doing them a favor. They seem appreciative of our benevolent attempts to control things for their benefit.

Because of the bent life resulting from the fall, life is filled with disappointment. It hurts. There are fears we can't articulate and never seem to conquer. Most things fail to deliver what they promise.

Marriage, which promises happily ever after, can quickly become a house of horror. Church life, which offers the possibility of community and grace, can deal unbelievable pain and disappointment.

It is not difficult to become cynical and jaded. Instead of being like the child who wakes wide-eyed on Christmas morning expecting to see the big presents from Santa's visit, we become critics of all mystery and judges of those who dare to risk believing the miraculous.

When God won't stay in our box, at best we're irritated and at worse, we're devastated.

Brandon had seen God answer prayers before. When his wife was diagnosed with cancer, he gathered his Christian friends around him and, with bolstered faith, he was sure God would heal her. For months they prayed. Many came with encouraging words and prophecies. They expected a miracle right up until her death.

The funeral was over, and the friends were gone. Alone with disappointment, Brandon decided it was all a farce. God had not come through for him. Maybe all the Bible stuff was as unreliable as His healing miracles.

He began to look outside the Christian community for his friends and fun. He met a woman who gave him special attention. She was married, but maybe that was another of those pointless rules in God's restrictive code.

God hadn't worked for him. Why should he work for God?

Brandon acted confident, brazen even. He had been freed from the restraining rules of religion and was now confident in his liberation. He based all of his decisions on what made him happy in the moment. But it was all a façade; all those who really knew him noticed that even his happiness was sad. They grieved the loss of the wide-eyed child of God who was willing to risk because of his trust in the goodness God.

This story is not new. It could be told by all of us.

As one writer stated during an Easter celebration, we are called to live as Easter people in a Good Friday world.

Life is painful at times but always redeemable. The gospel of Jesus promises us that nothing outside of His control will ever touch us and that all things will be woven into a tapestry that glorifies the Son.

When our pain is greater than our desire to glorify Him, we all fall prey to anger and disappointment. That alone doesn't disqualify us for redemption. In fact, it is much better than retreating into a religious rebellion that refuses to acknowledge pain and covers it with Bible verses and church activities.

God never seems upset with our honest complaints about His sovereignty. He has provided grace for hurting people. He gets to show one of His favorite traits when we come to Him in need.

He is full of mercy. And it's new every morning.

There's no mercy in religion. It's common for people who define life by rules and moral codes to simplify life when it hurts too much—they're looking to assign blame and find fault. They can't accuse God, so they either become bitter against the one who hurt them or they turn to penance to make restitution.

Confidence in religion is incapable of producing confidence before God. You'll never be able to do enough. And in the process, all the energy that God gives us to enjoy life and live it to the fullest is wasted in the ugly self-righteousness that makes them despise their neighbor and keeps them far from God.

You don't dream when you're self-righteous. Religion doesn't allow you to dream, it fills you with fear of punishment instead of hope that comes from faith.

But when you put your trust in God, when your faith is in Him and not in your ability to understand why things happened the way they did, you will have confidence before God!

Confidence before God is only found "in Christ." We have it because we know that He has it and He gives it to us— nothing more, nothing less.

Hebrews encourages us with the confidence we have in Christ.

> . . . but Christ is faithful over God's house as a son. And we are his house if indeed we hold fast our confidence and our boasting in our hope (Hebrews 3:6).

The context here is the contrast of the old covenant and the new, the old house and the new. Moses' house was the nation of Israel and its culture. Moses, as great as he was, only represented a servant in the house. Jesus is the Son in the house, and we are part of the new order of things.

In the past, the best we could hope for was to be a servant. Now God calls us "sons." If you read the way the Bible talks about God's relationship with Moses, it's a big deal to say we can be closer to God than he was.

Greater than Moses! Not bad.

Think of it this way. You probably wouldn't just walk into your boss' house unannounced and boldly ask him for something. You're relationship isn't that close; you don't have that kind of confidence.

But you'd be a lot more likely to walk into your dad's house without thinking twice. When you know you're welcomed and loved, it fills you with confidence.

In Moses' house the focus was on laws, land, temple, and city. In the new house the focus is on Spirit, resurrection, church, and world. Our inheritance is more than land. We get everything from God in Christ.

> Let us then with confidence draw near to the throne of grace, that we may receive mercy and find grace to help in time of need (Hebrews 4:16).

The subject here is the confidence we have because Jesus is the final high priest. He has made the eternal sacrifice and stands as the everlasting priest before God on our behalf. We are qualified before God because of the completion of Jesus' priestly work. He took care of everything. Our debt has been paid, and we are welcomed into the presence of God; we're not just allowed, we're invited. *"Therefore do not throw away your confidence, which has a great reward"* (Hebrews 10:35).

The reward of our confidence is the strength to persevere through all adversity and hardship. We can rest assured that God will ultimately vindicate His plan and justice will be final.

Over and over God has demonstrated His faithfulness. He has given us this confidence by raising Jesus from the dead. The down payment of His Holy Spirit guarantees the success of His redemptive plan where all things will be put to rights.

Jesus promised during His stay on earth that the enemies of His people would be judged in that generation. They were. In 70 AD, the unbelieving Jews were destroyed by the Romans. Later, the Romans were destroyed.

One day *all* the enemies will be exposed and justice will reign because the Judge has already come.

When the delays seem never-ending and injustice seems to be inevitable, we need confidence that time is only serving the purposes of God who has guaranteed redemption. While we wait for His ruling, we can enjoy the outpouring of *agape* as the power of the cross turns enemies into disciples of Jesus.

We have the confidence that God loves us and that we can love with His power. Like children on Christmas morning, we can wake each day with the wide-eyed expectation that God will confirm our message and mission with accompanying signs. Confidence before God has been restored as we are reconciled to God.

We are free to be the men God created us to be—confident men comfortable in their own skin.

FOR FURTHER STUDY

1. Do you have the confidence from God described in 1 John 3:18-24? What keeps you from having that kind of confidence? What strengthens it?

2. What kind of confidence was Paul talking about in 2 Corinthians 3? Where does it come from? How does that kind of confidence change your life?

3. Are there areas of your life where you still struggle with shame and condemnation? What can you do to fill that part of your soul with the confidence of God?

4. Name a specific area of your life where you need the confidence of God. How do you think God wants you to feel about it? Describe what it would look like to be confident.

CHAPTER
MEN AND THEIR TOOLS
THIRTEEN

When I finished my studies in seminary, several of my fellow students were complaining about how disappointed they were with their experience. They wanted seminary to prepare them for every eventuality they would face in the future.

Somehow they expected their education to fill them with all the knowledge and inspiration necessary to passionately minister for God.

What they had been given instead were some essential tools and the invitation to go and learn how to minister on the job.

I distinctly remember the day I received my private plane pilot's license. After the test flight with the instructor, he signed the license and slid it toward me with these words: "Now, go learn to fly."

In both of these situations the goal was not an exhaustive education; it was to give you enough of the skills to go out and get the job done.

I think that's basically the same approach Jesus took with His disciples.

These 12 men who spent three years with Jesus were released long before they fully understood what they were getting into. They had been given some indispensable tools during their training, but they didn't even know what they were all for.

Through the pages of Acts, we see them trying out their tools and getting better at using them skillfully and effectively through trial and error. They learned on the job.

I fear that most of those disciples would not have passed our "discipleship course" in many churches. We never would have trusted them in our congregations, but Jesus chose to build His church on their best efforts and many mistakes.

They still had some rough spots and didn't fully understand their mission (note their question in Acts 1:6 and the many changes they experience up through Acts 15). But they weren't defeated by failure, and they ultimately changed their world.

As I mentioned earlier, we have created an atmosphere in the contemporary church that is more conducive to being nurtured than being empowered. I think it's significant that some mega-churches are now admitting that their strategy to provide programs for every expressed need of the congregation is not making disciples.

People who have attended the classes and embraced the church vision still can't live productively and effectively in the world. They struggle with ethics. They don't know how to apply moral values to everyday decisions or even determine what moral values are. They are prone to debt, deception, and depression.

Too many depend on their preacher to tell them what to do spiritually, their lawyer to instruct them on ethics, their counselor to tell them how to cope with their psychological issues, and the media to inform them on public policy.

The shortcomings of this approach are obvious, as Christians are unnecessarily tossed back and forth as immature and ungrounded followers instead of strong leaders.

In comparison, the methods of Jesus shine brightly, providing wisdom and blessing for all those willing to obey. Wisdom doesn't have to shout; its superiority is obvious to all. Instead of building His church on a corporate model, He focuses on a few essential tools for His followers.

First, He provides them with constant fellowship with Himself:

> "If you love me, you will keep my commandments. And I will ask the Father, and he will give you another Helper, to be with you forever, even the Spirit of truth, whom the world cannot receive, because it neither sees him nor knows him. You know him, for he dwells with you and will be in you" (John 14:15-17).

We should consider getting rid of the language we use that reflects partial fellowship with God. It might be comfortable, but it's not really true. Here's just a few:

"God was really with me today."

"I loved that church service. God was there today."

"God is so far away from me right now."

"I have walked away from God and need to get back."

"I'm doing all I can to get closer to God."

The truth is, when we come to God through faith in Jesus, we are united with Him by His indwelling Spirit. He indicated to the original disciples what it would be like after His resurrection: *"In that day you will know that I am in my Father, and you in me, and I in you"* (John 14:20).

When we realize that God has given us the privilege of living in His constant presence, we'll never be the same. It makes life totally different. He is our ever present help in times of need. He'll never leave us or forsake us.

He enjoys our company and constantly grants us His wisdom and perspective on our situation. He fully satisfies every longing in us that cries out for intimacy.

And when we are aware of His presence, we aren't as likely to engage in activities that offend Him. As we learn to discern His voice we realize we have divine wisdom available to us at all times. He speaks to us by the "inner witness" of His presence.

Living in communion with Christ is the key to effective living. What a privilege!

> If then you have been raised with Christ, seek the things that are above, where Christ is, seated at the right hand of God. Set your minds on things that are

above, not on things that are on earth. For you have died, and your life is hidden with Christ in God (Colossians 3:1-3).

When we ignore this and try to live for Him without His presence, we find it tiring and non-productive. We are doomed to stumble trying to live this way, but the good news is God keeps no record of our missteps.

We are being trusted and trained.

The second essential tool is a Christ-centered approach to interpreting Scripture, which is the foundation for all wisdom and knowledge. I mentioned this in an earlier chapter.

A priority for Jesus after His crucifixion and resurrection was instructing His original disciples in a lesson on interpreting Old Testament scriptures. You can read the story of the walking lesson on "The Emmaus Road" in the twenty-fourth chapter of Luke's Gospel.

As Jesus walks with two of His followers, He listens to them describe their pain before He encourages them through interpreting all the scriptures concerning Him. He does the same thing later when He meets with a larger group of His disciples.

Can you imagine what those Bible studies must have been like?

They didn't just learn information—the disciples passionately described their experience with the question:

"Did not our hearts burn within us . . . while he opened to us the Scriptures?" (Matthew 24:32).

I am afraid that most Bible studies don't have that effect. In fact, the Scriptures have been used and abused to lend authority to many wrong doctrines.

One thing we can be sure of is that since history is about Jesus, and the Scripture is God's perspective on history, Scripture is about Jesus. Whatever other benefits we might gain from studying them, the main focus is the centrality of Christ. All ideas, concepts, beliefs, and doctrines must be filtered through the message of the cross.

This is why Paul made the decision to preach nothing but this message and interpret everything in light of it:

> And I, when I came to you, brothers did not come proclaiming to you the testimony of God with lofty speech or wisdom. For I decided to know nothing among you except Jesus Christ and him crucified. And I was with you in weakness and in fear and much trembling, and my speech and my message were not in plausible words of wisdom, but in demonstration of the Spirit and of power, that your faith might not rest in the wisdom of men but in the power of God (1 Corinthians 2:1-5).

On behalf of all of us in church leadership, I want to apologize to you men who have not been taught this perspective in studying the Bible.

Many of you have felt incompetent, unqualified, or inadequate to personally study the Scriptures. We've blown it on both sides; either we made the Bible too complicated and unapproachable or we over-simplified God's Word and underestimated its value.

Please forgive us, and let's now get serious about approaching the Scriptures the way Jesus did. In every passage, we relate it to Jesus. Once we understand how it relates to Christ, we can then apply it to our lives through Him.

The Bible illuminates every detail of our lives when we see it properly. It doesn't tell us what decision to make in every instance, but it gives us the perspective to make that decision with confidence in His wisdom.

The third essential tool is a biblical framework for making decisions and interpreting culture. Some would call this "a Christian worldview." As we seek to be good managers of God's creation and especially of our particular assignment, we must know how to identify what we are managing and make wise decisions.

Remember, God gave Adam the ability to name the animals in his stewardship of the earth. That means he had the capacity to see the true nature of things and manage accordingly.

It has been said that if you confuse an alligator for a poodle, you might lose your leg trying to pet it.

Many men are confused about trying to manage their stuff because they haven't discerned the true nature of people and things. The key to regaining that skill is to properly recognize God as God and give Him proper thanks. When mankind has refused to do that, they have gotten confused as to the nature of Creator and created, men and women, and truth as it differs from error (Romans 1:18-32).

With so many ideas, values, and agendas vying for influence and followers in our world, we need some tools for evaluation. All communication that we interact with, whether through television, music, books, conversations and public opinion, theater, pulpit, or podium, must be evaluated by some common criteria:

(1) What does it say about ultimate reality? In other words, how did we get here, where are we going, and why?

The answer to these fundamental questions defines our notion of God or the divine.

(2) What is our great dilemma? What is the nature of evil, and where does it come from?

The answer to this reveals the diagnosis of the underlying problem of mankind. Is it sin? Is it lack of time for evolution to work? Is it man's intrusion on nature? Is it that as humans we are fractured from the universal but impersonal nirvana?

(3) What is the real solution? Where do we look for hope?

The answer will reveal what strategy is being used to remedy the problems we face. Do we need a Savior? If so, who? Do we need to get rid of religion so mankind can save itself?

Skillfully using these tools requires time, training, and practice. At our house we engage in movie analysis together. Often after watching a movie together we take the time to discuss how the film affected us. It's not always easy, and it requires time and energy, but the more we do it, the more aware we are of these powerful and influential messages.

Some inspire us, some discourage us, but in time, none of them will go unnoticed.

The fourth essential tool is a vital connection with the community of faith, the local church. The Christian life cannot be lived effectively alone as we have noted in a previous chapter. We must find our place in the body of Christ and contribute to the team. Those who try it alone will inevitably be disappointed.

Those who engage will find it challenging but worth every bump.

We hear God through the gifted brothers and sisters that make up our faith community. They each have different gifts and perspectives on life that can help us make wise decisions. We have mentors and peers that have the right to speak in to our lives, and we are foolish to ignore them when guidance is needed.

There is so much that could be said about these tools, and my temptation is to continue writing in order to prepare you for every eventuality in the future. But just as it did for my friends at seminary, that approach would miss the point.

Men like to be trusted with projects that call out their creativity and demand their commitment. You're going to learn on the job.

Here are your tools. Trial and error is part of the process of spiritual development. Gratitude and perseverance are manly.

I suggest you evaluate your tool chest. What do you have, and what are you lacking?

The project of bringing God's kingdom on earth is calling. It's time to get on with the task and start using them. Sure, there's risk involved, but there is excitement in risk.

It is what you were created and redeemed for. You know and enjoy who God made you.

You are a man comfortable in your own skin.

FOR FURTHER STUDY

1. What is our assignment as Christians? (Here's a hint: Genesis 1:26-28, Matthew 28:18-20)

2. What are the essential tools for the job? Do you have these tools in your chest?

3. How do you plan to get on with the task? Be specific.

APPENDIX I
ADDITIONAL RESOURCES

FOR FURTHER READING:

Why Men Hate Going to Church by David Morrow
Morrow's book is an eye-opening study of the reasons why so many men don't go to church.

Grace Works by Dudley Hall
This book exposes the inadequacy of religion and offers the true hope found in a vital relationship with God.

Incense and Thunder by Dudley Hall
This is a great resource to help you understand how to pray from the divine perspective. We're most effective in our prayer life when we approach prayer as a lifestyle. It also includes specific suggestions on how to pray for estranged children.

Agape Road by Bob Mumford
In order for us to be in right relationship with God, we've got to understand His heart. Bob does a great job describing the difference between self love and God-like love.

The Search for Significance by Robert McGee
McGee's book has helped many people by clearly exposing the lies that paralyze us. God's love gives us significance apart from anything we ever do. Our performance can't earn God's love.

Healing The Masculine Soul by Gordon Dalbey
So many men are wounded and need healing in their soul. Dalbey does an excellent job identifying and addressing the man-wound that all men must overcome.

Shame Off You by Alan Wright
This book gets to the heart of what causes men to shy away from their masculinity. It's the best book on shame I've ever read.

For Further Study:

Heart Burn by Dudley Hall
This audio/video series will show you how to interpret Scripture from a Christ-centered perspective, the first step in sound Bible study.

Life as Discovery by Dudley Hall
All of us need to recognize and receive the grace of God in our lives on an ongoing basis. This audio series will teach you how to continually open the package of grace that God has given us.

Meaning in the Market Place by Dudley Hall
Building the Kingdom of God in the market place is a high calling that is worthy of honor. This audio series and accompanying workbook clarify the role of the market place minister, establish the foundations for a Christian work ethic, and explain how to give dignity and anointing to daily work.

Men Who Make a Difference by Dudley Hall
This 12-part audio series with workbook has been designed for men in small groups.

APPENDIX II

A SUGGESTED CURRICULUM FOR STARTING
A MEN'S DISCIPLESHIP GROUP

I. **Who are we?**
Premise: we ultimately act out of our true being.
"Behavior follows being."

1. **The importance of a name**
Genesis 1-2
God gives Adam the job and capacity to give people names to the animals. He could discover the nature of things he was to manage. Our success at stewardship depends on our ability to accurately discover the true nature of the people with whom we relate and the things we are to manage.

2. **The nature of wisdom**
Proverbs 1-5
1) Wisdom is a divine perspective on people and things.
2) Man's fall affected his perspective—he became self-obsessed.
3) In Solomon we see a type of the ultimate wisdom in Christ.
4) In Proverbs we find practical conclusions based on wisdom.
5) Ecclesiastes shows us a perspective of life when the divine perspective is missing.
6) Jesus is ultimate wisdom (1 Corinthians 1:30-31).
7) Wisdom is available to us (James 1:1-5).

3. **The divine perspective of our identity**
1) We are children of Abraham (Galatians 3:10-14).
2) We are children of God (John 1:12).
3) We are ambassadors (2 Corinthians 5:20).
4) We are servants of the King (2 Timothy 2:24-26).
5) We are believers (John 6:29).
6) We are witnesses (Acts 1:8).
7) We are the temple (1 Corinthians 6:19).

4. The lies that must be exposed and replaced with truth
    1) You are what you do — truth: you do what you are.
    2) You are what others say — God has a right to name you.
    3) Your nature is permanent — Resurrection can change you.

II. What is our assignment?

Premise: We are significant because God personally created us and purposefully equipped each of us to fulfill our role in His overall plan.

1. What is the original mandate?
Genesis 1:26-28
    1) What did "subdue" look like to Adam?
       • To Moses?
       • To David?
       • To Jesus?
       • To us?
    2) What interfered with mankind's ability to fulfill his destiny? (Romans 3:23) (Genesis 3)
    3) How is that obstacle addressed in the Christ-event?

2. What is the subsequent mandate?
Matthew 28:18-20
    1) How does making disciples relate to subduing the earth?
    2) How does the concept of clergy and laity relate to both mandates?
    3) How does your vocation relate to each mandate?
    4) What do you need to help you align your vocation with God's assignment to us all?

III. What are our tools for work?
Premise: God equips those He calls.

1. Jesus demonstrated life as man can live (John 17). What does that mean to us?

2. **He featured** the open and continued fellowship He had with the Father (John 14-17). Is this possible for us? How?

3. **He made** a priority of showing His disciples how to interpret Scripture (Luke 24:13-49). What can you do to gain this skill?

4. **He demonstrated** a love-motivated ethic by rejecting lifeless religious form while embracing a single focused life for the glory of His Father (Luke 10:25-37). What is the basis of your decision making?

5. **He showed** the importance of interpreting the "times." Are you aware of what your culture is communicating through movies, music, and media? What do you need to gain competence in this?

6. **He has given** us the Holy Spirit (John 14). How do we embrace this gift? (1 Corinthians 12-14)

7. **He modeled** discipleship by forming a small group of mutually submissive learners who would be equipped, released, and sustained. How are you following that model?

IV. **How do we manage our lives?**
Premise: "Subduing" involves managing.

1. **You fix things, and you bless people.**
   People respond to affirmation, encouragement, and clear direction. They react to being fixed like a broken refrigerator. (Review some of the 30+ reciprocal commands in the New Testament. Example: 1 Thessalonians 5:12-19 and Galatians 6:1-10.)

2. **We live for the purpose of glorifying God.**
   In 1 Corinthians 8-10 there are some guidelines for decision-making.
   • What are they?
   • How can you apply those to your own situation?

3. **Money is either a tool or an idol.**
   2 Corinthians 8-9 gives some excellent guidelines for handling money. Also review 1 Timothy 6:11-20.
   - Does your financial history reveal that your goal is to be a giver?

4. **Your appetites (desires) serve you, or you serve them.**
   James 4:1-10 is instructive about our desires.
   - How can you apply this to you?
   - 1 Thessalonians 4:1-11 describes a life under control. What hope do you find there that you can be that free?

5. **Your responsibilities go beyond you.**
   Matthew 28:18-20
   It is our privilege to affect our culture with the power of Christ's Kingdom. What is your Christian responsibility as:
   - A husband?
   - A father?
   - A church member?
   - A citizen of your city, state, nation, world?

6. **Your gifts qualify you as a team member.**
   We don't need a team if our vision is so small we can fulfill it alone.
   - What is your vision for your life?
   - What are you assigned to affect for God's glory?
   - What gifts have you identified in your own life?
   - What other gifts do you need in order to accomplish your goals?
   - Where will you find those gifts?
   - What are the different teams you are a part of now?
   - What is your role in each?

Appendix III
"RITES OF PASSAGE"

Every boy needs to know when he is a man. Otherwise, he will spend too much time and energy trying to live up to false roles of what he thinks a man is: a great athlete, a reckless rebel, a successful businessman, or a powerful politician. He needs affirmation that he has become a man, and that comes from one place—a father.

We have designed a father and son weekend around a "Rites of Passage" that facilitates a community of men supporting a father calling his son into the pursuit of the ideals of manhood and affirming him as a member of the community of men. That may be a mouthful, but it captures the critical elements of the Rites of Passage.

FIRST, it is a community. Sure, a father can affirm his son one-on-one, but in the presence of a community it takes on added power and significance. There is encouragement and a greater sense of affirmation and recognition. As we said before, a man in isolation is in danger. The presence of the community also provides the support needed by a young man whose natural father is absent. These men especially need the community to step up and fill the father gap. The role of the community is critical.

SECOND, the father calls his son into the pursuit of the ideals of manhood. Going through the ceremony doesn't make you a perfect man. It doesn't mean you don't screw up. If that were the case none of us would qualify. It means that you commit yourself to becoming the highest ideal of man you possibly can, that you dedicate yourself to conform to the image of Christ. You make your decisions to the best of your ability with that goal in mind. We build of our retreat around three "Marks of Manhood"—*integrity, responsibility and accountability* as described throughout this book.

THIRD, the father affirms his son as a member of the community of men. The father tells both his son and the community of men that he is proud of the man his son has become. This changes the relationship between the son and friends of the father. The son is now a man and a peer in the community. This does not mean that the father is no longer a God-ordained authority or that the son shouldn't show respect and honor to his father and to his father's friends. But it does mean the son relates to the community on a man-to-man basis.

FINALLY, there are the Rites of Passage and the ceremony itself. We make a pretty big deal of the ceremony at our retreat—using dozens of tiki torches, blind-folds, and trust walks, taking advantage of the natural environment as best we can. I suppose it is possible for the ceremony to be too elaborate, but that's an extreme I find rare in the pragmatic culture we live in.

The purpose of the ceremony is to etch the mental and emotional mile-stone in the memory of each young man. The ceremony drives the stake into the ground and says, "This is when and where it happened."

That's why the more memorable the ceremony, the better. We do everything we can to make these Rites of Passage a defining moment in the life of a young man, a moment he'll never forget. It's a critical moment both for the young men and the community itself. I encourage you to establish this process in your community of men.

ACKNOWLEDGEMENTS

I owe a great debt to the thousands of hungry men who have pushed me to deal with the issues we face.

What would I do without the generous love and expert advice of my dear friend Dr. Glenda Williams? She takes my words and actually makes them say something.

It has been a pleasure working with Inprov, Ltd. Jimmy James and Terry Redmon have been faithful friends and helpful supporters for a long time. Their staff, especially Jed Walker, was very helpful, and it was fun to work with them.

Thanks!!